D0762519

The Ogoki River Guides

Emergent Leadership Among the Northern Ojibwa

Edward J. Hedican

The Ogoki River Guides

Emergent Leadership
Among the
Northern
Ojibwa

Edward J. Hedican

Wilfrid Laurier University Press

Canadian Cataloguing
in Publication Data

Hedican, Edward J.
    The Ogoki River Guides

Bibliography: p.
Includes index.
ISBN 0-88920-199-4

1. Ogoki River Guides Ltd.   2. Indians of North
America — Ontario — Collins (Post office) —
Business enterprises.   3. Métis — Ontario — Collins
(Post office) — Business enterprises.*   4. Ojibwa
Indians — Government relations.*   5. Métis —
Ontario — Collins (Post office) — Government rela-
tions.*   6. Indians of North America — Canada —
Government relations.   7. Collins (Ont. : Post
office) — Commerce.   I. Title.

E99.C6H43 1986   971.3'12   C86-094970-2

Copyright © 1986

WILFRID LAURIER UNIVERSITY PRESS
Waterloo, Ontario, Canada   N2L 3C5

Cover design by Polygon Design Limited

Printed in Canada

*For Mary-Ann, Shaun, Tara,
and my parents*

Contents

List of Maps and Figures

Maps

Figures

List of Tables

Acknowledgments

In the process of researching and writing this book, I have come to owe a great deal to many people. Here I would like to express my grateful acknowledgment for the assistance which I have received in carrying out this task. Almost everyone in the Collins community has helped me out at one time or another with food, travel, friendship, and information, among other things. It is not possible to mention them all individually, but to each I remain grateful for their time, assistance, and unselfish co-operation. Those who contributed the most to my well-being in the field and the data necessary for the successful completion of this project were Annie Basketwang, Samson Basketwang, Steve Goodwin, Josie Kwandibens, Peter Kwandibens, Canon John Long, Vaino (Montreal) Paavola, Donald Patience, Dorothy Patience, Elizabeth Patience, Hamish Patience, Peter Patience, Steve Quisses, Sogo Sabosons, Linda Staats, Tom Wastaken, and Sinclair Wynn.

In academic circles there are many people who have been particularly helpful in providing support and encouragement during the course of the research, or in providing comments on various drafts of the manuscript, in particular, Don Attwood, Ken Dawson, Ken Duncan, Carmen Lambert, Ken Menzies, Ed Rogers, Richard Salisbury, Philip Salzman, Frans Schryer, Peter Sindell, and Steve Strong. In addition, I am indebted to my brother Wil Hedican, a former school teacher at Collins, Weagamow (Round) Lake, Fort Hope, Fort Severn, and elsewhere, for providing numerous insights into northern village life over the years. I also owe an immeasurable debt to Mary-Ann Cheesequay, a childhood resident of Collins, for her continuing encouragement.

The field work on which this book is based was supported by a grant from the Centre for Northern Studies and Research, McGill University, Montreal. Further financial assistance was provided by the McGill Programme in the Anthropology of Development and the Canada Council, in the form of a Doctoral Fellowship. This book has been published with the help of a grant from the Social Science Federation of Canada, using funds provided by the Social Sciences and Humanities Research Council of Canada. However none of these individuals or agencies should be held responsible for any deficiencies or opinions expressed in this study, which remain my responsibility alone. This work is dedicated to the memories of Raymond Wabasons, Harry Achnepeneeskum, and Elijah Yellowhead.

Preface

Collins is an Indian and Métis community of one hundred and fifty people situated in the spruce/pine forest belt of northern Ontario. It is not a town in the usual sense of the word. There is a large clearing between the store and the railway tracks where people occasionally congregate, but their houses are widely scattered in the surrounding bush. To visit someone you have to travel down sandy paths through stands of tall jack pine. Walking down these paths gives a sense of distance between people, as if this was not really a "community" at all, but a group of people accidently living in the same location. I have since come to regard such impressions with scepticism. There is a sense of community in Collins; it is just that Collins people do not like to live crammed together, or to adopt all the ways of the outside world. Most of all, it is not another so-called "dying Indian community."

Since the early 1970s Collins people have tried to take charge of their own affairs. Led by three Métis, sons of the village's former fur trader, the people have founded a locally operated tourist operation called Ogoki River Guides Ltd. The struggles of people in this organization to create a viable local economy has an important lesson for governmental policy in northern areas—people do not want their affairs controlled from the outside. They want to participate directly in the important decisions affecting their lives, and not as passive "target populations." Changes in current government practices are needed, especially in areas of local inputs into policy and control issues, if community-based groups like the Ogoki River Guides are to flourish and if real local initiative in economic development has a chance of becoming a widespread pattern.

It is therefore suggested that studies such as the present one which focus on the economic development projects of the native community are necessary in order to help orient government policy and planning. The problem is that the literature in the area of native development programs is particularly sparce, thus hindering efforts aimed at making accurate comparisons and reaching informed conclusions. Jorgensen (1971), for example, studied how Shoshone and Ute Indians adapt to the stresses produced when they are denied access to crucial political, social, and economic resources, and reveals how American Indians in rural areas are pressed into states of underdevelopment by the multiple influences of metropolitan political economies. But is the political economy of the large urban centre to be seen as the sole source of difficulty for the native community? A study of a furniture factory project on the Cape Croker Reserve in Ontario suggests that both government and local people must share in the responsibility for failure (Duran and Duran 1973). In the Cape Croker case an attempt to establish a cedar furniture factory on the reserve ran into difficulty because local people lacked the managerial experience to compete in the highly competitive furniture industry. For the government's part the Indian Affairs Branch was not properly equipped in terms of adequate resources and trained personnel to handle economic development projects in the native community. By contrast, development projects among the Menomini (Spindler and Spindler 1971) and Fox Indians (Gearing 1960) have been successful ventures because of the managerial and executive skills of the local population, in conjunction with effective outside aid. More studies such as these are needed if successful development activity in the native community is to be promoted.

Besides changes in government dealings with native communities, a second theme of this study centres around the fact that Collins is not a federal Indian reserve. Such "non-reserves" do not come under the jurisdiction of the Department of Indian Affairs and Northern Development (DIAND), but are administered by provincial governments. This research on the Collins community is therefore seen as a unique opportunity to study local political and economic development outside the DIAND administrative framework. The situation of ineffectual leadership on DIAND-administered reserves is well documented, but what sort of leaders emerge in native communities not constrained by DIAND guidelines? What are non-reserve leaders' goals, methods, and motivations? Questions such as these have led me to regard the non-reserve native community as an important category apart from federally-administered reserves because of fundamental differences between the two types of native community in terms of their relationships with the larger Canadian society. An ethnographic literature in which only reserve communities are studied is one-sided and incomplete.

CHAPTER ONE

Introduction

This study is about the evolution of economic and political behaviour in the non-reserve Indian community of Collins, Ontario. In particular, *The Ogoki River Guides* documents an unusual case in emergent Ojibwa leadership. Surrounded by settlements with chronic unemployment and welfare dependency, the Collins community has made a start in another direction. Collins people have embarked on a long-term plan to revitalize their community and to survive in a post-trapping world. To facilitate this goal, a village-wide corporation—Ogoki River Guides Ltd. (ORG)—was established to implement and direct an ambitious socio-economic program. Throughout the 1970s Collins leaders employed an effective strategy for generating outside financial aid, and are striving to build a million-dollar tourist industry upon which rests their collective hopes for future economic viability.

Collins is moreover significant because it is a "non-reserve" Indian settlement, which means that it is not supported financially or otherwise by the Department of Indian Affairs and Northern Development (DIAND) in Ottawa. Thus, this facet of the study allows us to examine local-level development outside the DIAND administrative framework. Given the dearth of literature on the subject of economic and political development in non-reserve communities in the North, we are led to ask about the nature of leadership in such settlements. Are leaders elected as they are on most reserves? Do leaders hold their positions by consensus, or perhaps by domination? Is their basis of community support a wide or narrow one? Since non-reserves are outside the DIAND aid program, does the provincial government fill the void in community services? Are non-reserves less or more successful at securing jobs for workers than reserves? These questions indicate that there is an important reason for considering non-reserves as a category apart from DIAND-administered reserves—there are fundamental differences between the two types of Indian community in terms of their relationship with the larger Canadian society.

1

The Research Problem

When European fur traders, missionaries, and soldiers made their initial contacts with the aboriginal people of North America they were impressed by the apparent lack of a recognizable authority structure in many Indian societies (Miller 1955). These early visitors saw a contradiction in the fact that Indians could organize large-scale collective efforts, as they did during buffalo drives on the plains or fishing on the west coast, without a strict hierarchy of leadership roles. Conversely, Indians had difficulty in understanding how someone could retain self-esteem, and much-valued individual autonomy, while at the same time accepting without question the directives or orders of many other people. If Indians saw European-style leadership as ruthless and demeaning, then Europeans tended to see Indian leaders, in general terms, as weak and ineffectual. It is evident that both Indians and Europeans had their own particular conceptions of leadership, power, and consent. One result of this situation is that whites in North America have not expended a great deal of effort in understanding the characteristics and processes of Indian leadership. It is not surprising then that whites have spent the last three centuries trying to change Indian leadership so that it would conform to the political norms and values characteristic of European cultural tradition.

Following the earlier efforts of their British and French predecessors, the Canadian government recognized the strategic importance of negotiating treaties with various native populations. In the northern regions alone some one-and-a-half million square miles of land has already been ceded to the government, and there are still vast areas, especially in the arctic and Northwest Territories, where treaties have never been negotiated. Indian land cessions allowed for more rapid settlement and development, and after a particular treaty was signed the government felt justified in attempts to convince Indians that they were now permanently under Canadian jurisdiction. In order to facilitate administrative control, special areas were set aside for Indian occupation and use and a system of elective local government was introduced. Via the Indian Act, the election of chiefs and councillors and their duties were specified.

The ethnographic literature documenting the effects of outside control over Indian communities tells us that if Indian leaders were weak in earlier times, then today they have lost even the last vestiges of local influence. We are told that the federal government imposed a political system that Indians have never understood, and therefore do not recognize (Landes 1937: 2-3). An Indian chief is called "boss-like" (*okima·hka·n*) among his own people—a surrogate for the real thing; and "put-up job" (Ellis 1960: 1). The chief and council are the least developed law-enforcing agency in Indian communities (Lips 1947: 475). Today's chief has even less power than was exercised by Indian leaders during the fur trade (Rogers 1965: 277). From available literature one conclusion predominates: in Indian communities "political sovereignty is attenuated, if not controlled ultimately by the Indian Affairs administration" (Dunning 1959a: 20). Similarly, Rogers (1965: 277) concludes that for Cree and Ojibwa leadership "the government asserts that authority be vested in the chief whereby he can carry out his duties. But in the final analysis, the chief has lost his former powers and acquired no new ones." Rogers then goes on to indicate that the chief has lost his former powers because he no longer has the multiplicity of role attributes that bolstered his position in former times—missionaries have taken over religious power in the band, the chief is no longer the main distributor of goods to band members, and many communities are divided by factional disputes.

But why has the chief acquired no new powers? A partial answer is that because of his tenuous hold on office, the chief is apt to avoid raising issues which could jeopardize his election chances. A chief also has a diminished role to play in community affairs because individuals can often by-pass the chief and consult directly with outside authorities, thus circumventing the chief's local basis of power and support. Another reason is that when a chief is in opposition to government policy he can be ignored by the officials attempting to implement these policies. In other words, the chief faces a steady erosion of power and influence from both inside and outside the community. As Brody (1975: 196) relates, "White officials expect the men to take prominent positions in local government institutions. But since these positions are seen to be devoid of power, the men who occupy them are criticized as ineffective. . . . Some men refuse to accept positions of 'authority' for precisely that reason: to accept is to become a target for criticism and ridicule."

We could go on here and discuss additional commentary on Indian leadership, but the results would not differ significantly from that summarized above. It is not my purpose to question the validity of the above reports, because as descriptions of particular events or circumstances there is no reason to question their accuracy, but I remain uneasy about the generalizations conveyed in these studies. Are there no strong Indian leaders or political organizations at the local level in Canada? What is the evidence that Indian people themselves see the exercise of leadership as futile and demeaning activities? Is it not possible that weak leadership is not so much a general characteristic of Indian communities, but a characteristic of communities singled-out for intensive study, ones with particular ties to the outside society that are not shared by other, less studied, communities?

Ethnography and Theory

The line of reasoning outlined by these questions led to my initial interest in the "non-reserve" (i.e., outside DIAND's jurisdiction) Indian community as a meaningful unit of study. My first chance to visit such a community came in 1971 when a school teacher in Collins, my brother, thought that, because of my anthropological interests, I might wish to stay for a few days. Travel to Collins was not all that difficult— three hours over a bumpy gravel road to the rail line, then a twenty minute train ride to the village. This first visit lasted not for a few days as expected, but for six weeks. It was not until 1974 that I returned, this time staying for a year, but the early trip was a valuable experience in terms of making friends and otherwise laying the ground work for further study. Right from the beginning I was intrigued with the main leaders in Collins. They were the sons of a Scottish fur trader who had quit the Hudson's Bay Company and started an independent store on the rail line. Many Indians, especially northerly ones dependent on the Hudson's Bay Company, gravitated to such locations because the independents offered high fur prices and inexpensive trade goods. The trader's three sons, after their father's death, started a vigorous community organization called Ogoki River Guides Ltd. to find jobs for Collins people and expand local services. In addition, the brothers have important family connections on their mother's side since her father was a chief still remembered as a negotiator of Treaty 9 in northern Ontario. Collins leaders were not the sort of passive, "surrogate for the real thing" people that might be expected. They had unusual qualities that made for effective local leadership. I wanted to find out why.

Collins leaders gained prominence quickly, and the organization they formed was a pivotal mechanism in uniting the people behind a common effort. Leaders used the organization to negotiate for government-funded work projects, and so were able to gain influence by dispensing jobs. In other words, there was a form of transaction or exchange occurring such that economic benefits were translated into local political support. This situation suggested that a focus on leaders as local patrons and social activators could serve as a general model for explaining economic and political change in the community. For example, a study of political organization in Pakistan notes that "persons find their place in the political order through a series of choices, many of which are temporary and revocable. The authority of a chief depends . . . on the mandate he is able, at any given time, to wrest from each of his followers individually" (Barth 1959: 2, 90). But politics is not simply a matter of "winners" having access to the largest or best resources, as indicated by the statement, "To be successful as a leader is to gain access to more resources than one's opponents" (Bailey

1969: 36). Equally important is how leaders use resources, and how they are able to manipulate them so as to attract and maintain a following. Patrons (a missionary and a storekeeper) in the Naskapi community studied by Henriksen (1971) had little local influence because they lacked control over economic resources. The store is run by the Newfoundland Government and so the Naskapi do not feel indebted to the storekeeper because they feel he is required to supply them with goods and see this as his function. Ironically, what little influence the missionary has stems from his intermediary role between the storekeeper and the Indians, who both need the priest as a translator. Thus, "the struggle for power between several middlemen of the same community . . . is an empirical matter relating to the assets the actors have at their disposal" (Henriksen 1971: 23).

In anthropology there are a number of other descriptions and analyses of patron roles that could be discussed (e.g., Boissevain 1966; Attwood 1974; Paine 1971). Most focus on the individual accumulation of clients, positions, or other assets. We are told, as in Paine's (1971: 14-15) work, how patrons initiate new kinds of transactions, but what is obscured by this individualistic or situational emphasis is the relationship between patrons' innovations and social change. Do the new kinds of transactions described by Paine and others have any long-lasting or generalizable effects on the local community? If patronage is a process linking local communities with state-supported institutions, then it is necessary to know more about patrons' strategies or innovations in terms of opportunities provided by the larger society, since neither the village nor the state in today's world is really a complete organization without the other.

Collins provided an ideal opportunity to study the activities of local patrons and mediators because government funding was used extensively to initiate economic change in the community. Thus, the theory adopted in this monograph is that Collins leaders gain influence by acting as intermediaries between government-supported funding agencies and the local population. In fact my argument is that the development of successful intermediary roles in Collins was a crucial factor not only in initiating economic change but in maintaining it throughout the 1970s. I doubt whether there would have been appreciable change in Collins without leaders capable of linking local aspirations with outside opportunities.

Does this mean that we can explain the emergence of a leader with an unusual capacity to organize people and resources in terms of his or her personality characteristics? In the beginning of my field work in Collins I thought that this was true. The literature on patrons and mediators placed a heavy emphasis on leadership as individual initiative, and descriptions of short term situations figured prominently in my early notes. However, I have now come to see this individualistic and situational emphasis as one of the methodological pitfalls of patronage studies—there is a tendency to reduce the explanation of social change to the personality level. It was only after I began to study the behaviour of Collins leaders in a wider historical and socio-economic context that my perspective began to change. My judgement now is that to try to account for the emergence of community leadership by personality or psychological traits alone yields only part of the answer. Accordingly, special attention is given in the present study to the following factors which, it is argued, in combination with one another provide a far more substantial explanation for the emergent leadership in Collins.

The first of these factors is that the present leaders of Collins have built on the earlier efforts of the Scottish trader to centralize power and authority in the village. The Ogoki River Guides emerged not at a time of socio-political chaos, but when much of the village's activities had already been focused around the trader's role as the community's main decision-maker. A second factor is the attempts by Collins leaders to formulate a long-term strategy for local development. With this strategy they could more effectively co-ordinate community efforts, develop an overall sense of commitment among community members, and conserve scarce resources. A careful distribution of economic benefits was a third factor facilitating the development of Collins leadership. Leaders made sure that as many people as possible were hired for particular projects, even if this meant that most had to work on a part-time basis. This wide distribution of economic rewards circumvented divisive tendencies in the community, and provided leaders with a supportive local following.

In sum, the aim of this study is to discuss and analyse the emergence of economic and political behaviour in the non-reserve Indian community of Collins. An exchange approach is adopted, such that Collins leaders are seen to gain power and influence through their intermediary role linking the local community with external agencies. A problem with previous studies of the patron role was noted, namely a tendency towards situational and psychological reductionism. A solution is offered such that the success of local patrons is seen in terms of historical and economic factors. In Collins these factors provided the conditions and opportunities for leaders to emerge. Without them even a forceful, charismatic leader would lack purpose.

Conditions of Field Work

The field work at Collins was carried out over a fifteen-month period. I arrived at Collins in the first week of July 1974. In October I left the field to do some more library research, and returned shortly after Christmas. The field trip ended with my departure from Collins at the end of October 1975. Previous to this time I had come to know several dozen Collins men who worked with me on tree planting projects during three summer periods (from 1969 to 1971). And, as mentioned earlier, six weeks were spent in Collins when I stayed with my brother, an adult education teacher. Since this period of field work I have returned to Collins just about every year, with visits ranging from a few days to a few weeks. The occasional letter or telephone call has also been exchanged with members of the community over this period.

During the first summer, in 1974, I had the good fortune of being able to occupy a small room attached to the home of one of the Collins leaders. He treated me like a guest of the household, providing me with meals and as much time for discussion as I wanted. Since this leader's house and adjacent store was also a centre of activity in the community, I was readily able to keep up with village affairs. Note keeping was a bit of a problem, because industriousness conflicted with my role as a guest, so I found myself frequenting the out-house more than usual where I would hastily jot down a page or two of observations. My unusual behaviour did not go unnoticed, however, since on one occasion the leader wanted to know if his wife's cooking had given me loose bowels. My explanation, that I was just taking notes, seemed to puzzle him even more.

When I returned the following Christmas I asked the leader if he would help me find my own place in which to live. His hospitality was appreciated, I explained, but I needed my own place to read, write, and entertain the occasional guest. He pointed his finger at a vacant log cabin a few hundred feet in front of his place, and suggested that I should see the owner about renting it. The owner agreed to let me stay in the cabin, but I had trouble talking to him about the rent. After several hours, and a round trip walk to his place of five miles, I began to realize that he was more interested in establishing ownership than in making a profit. Accordingly, he would stay at my place when he made a trip to town, and every once and a while I would slip him ten or twenty dollars, not as "rent," but as a token of his status as landlord. The cabin itself caused some unexpected problems. The wood stove was rotted out on the bottom and I would look up at night to watch the light emitted from these holes twinkle across the ceiling. I had to borrow a power saw to cut wood. But while I learned that foraging for wood was a strenuous and time-consuming activity, I found that I had no time, or energy, for note taking. The bucket of water I would place above the stove before going to bed would be frozen to the bottom by morning. I covered a four-foot hole in the wall (where a window used to be) with a sheet of plastic, which was scant protection from the thirty-degree-below weather outside. A neighbour came to the rescue with an oil stove, I sent out for a window, and with the coming of warmer weather I began to feel more at home. People would see me working on the cabin and would stop to chat, which gave me additional opportunities to gather information.

Informants

During my first couple of months in the cabin I found that I missed opportunities to ask important questions. Older people, friends of the owner, would see my light on in the evening and would stop in for a talk. Realizing that their friend was not there, the visitors would excuse themselves and walk away. I then set to work making a list of all the people that might pay a call under similar conditions. Beside each name I jotted down questions I could ask which would reveal to me the things they knew best, such as their knowledge about hunting, working on the railroad, or other activities. In this way I became better prepared for people's visits, casually conversing with them, without having to use formal interviews or structured questionnaires in informal situations.

I was determined to acquire as much knowledge about the local language as I could. Ojibwa was the usual language of conversation in the village. Most of the younger people could speak English, but I did not wish to miss the chance to listen to the older people. Arrangements were therefore made for a young man to give me lessons a couple times a week. I had a grammar and dictionary of Ojibwa and studied this for an hour each morning. Even with this effort I still feel inadequate in the use of the language, speaking in "Indian baby-talk," as one person remarked. On the whole, people tried to give me as much help as possible in using the language, even refusing to use English when they thought I should be able to follow along. Some of the older people were startled at times when I would speak to them in Ojibwa. I was told later that they thought it biologically impossible for white people to speak Indian, except for priests, who used religious power to accomplish the feat.

The children were perhaps easiest to get along with, and were usually eager sources of information on the things other people were trying to keep quiet. They also occasionally raided my pantry looking for cookies when I was away, so I tried to keep a step ahead of them by placing a few cookies on the bottom shelf which was easily reached from the door. At times they would try to torment me by jumping on the roof, or staring in the window, but I preferred to live with this than to chase them away.

Most of the time informants provided me with well-balanced material, which I usually tried to cross-check from other sources. But at other times my questioning led to unexpected situations. One afternoon I was asking a hunter about the number and kinds of animals he had trapped the previous winter. He gave me this information, but returned the same evening convinced that I was a game warden. After I asked a railway worker about his sources of income, he returned with his income tax form, thinking I served in some government capacity. Somewhat mystified, I filled it out for him and he seemed to go home satisfied. Several months later he knocked on my door and handed me five dollars. He explained that his income tax cheque had just arrived, and he was bringing over his fee. Refusing the money was useless, because then he would become suspicious about why I filled the form out in the first place.

With a total population of one hundred and fifty people, it is possible to become acquainted with just about everyone in the village. Visiting between households is a frequent activity of most people and I was usually expected to participate, although I was looking for the opportunity to join such activities in any event. I was also expected to share in material things, as they did, which sometimes conflicted with my personal preference. Nobody locked their doors, except occasionally at night. Knocking was also unknown, and people were accustomed to just opening the door and walking in. I found the temptation to knock hard to resist, but stopped when I learned that a knock on the door signalled a stranger.

Overall I would say that a use of informants provided the most comprehensive source of material, especially in the form of something new or unusual, for this study. Informants also provided the most significant insights derived from the field work, particularly when they discussed their feelings, thoughts, or attitudes.

Local Records

One of the important differences between a non-reserve community, such as Collins, and Indian reserves in terms of conducting research is that reserves have much more extensive records. For each reserve DIAND keeps records of band meetings, population changes, letters, and other material which are especially useful to the researcher in documenting various historical trends. Such records are not kept for Collins because it is outside DIAND's jurisdiction, but there is still some Indian Affairs material that was found useful in this study. Just over half of the population of Collins is composed of treaty Indians who are still recorded on various band lists even though they no longer live on a reserve. These band lists provided a useful checkpoint for verifying people's age, family relationships, and place of birth. Indian Affairs records of the location of families receiving treaty payments, as well as the trap line areas for various band members, were a valuable source of information for reconstructing aspects of the community's social and economic history.

Records have been kept at the local school house since its start in 1960. These were useful in determining when various families moved in and out of Collins, the length of time students spent on the trap line in winter, the rapid turnover of both students and teachers, as well as which families tended to stress educational achievement over others. The serendipitous comments that teachers make in the margins were an unexpected source of insights into students' relationships with one another, personality traits, and work habits.

I was also fortunate that the storekeeper allowed me to search through his files. These were used to find out such things as the quantity of food and goods consumed in the community, the extent of credit arrangements, and which families harvested the most furs. In an old storehouse I found a pile of bills from the early 1940s which were used to reconstruct Collins early population, and to determine long-term changes in consumer preference. A fur trader's record book from an even earlier period was located behind some old shelves. I was fascinated by this find because the trader's costs were written in code, something which took me weeks to unravel. He kept a complete list of trappers, the location of their trap lines, and the amount and kinds of furs traded. The price paid for these furs was written in capital letters, rather than numbers. He was obviously trying to keep the information a secret, but from whom—his competitors, or maybe game officials? While puzzling over the trader's code I was almost unwittingly drawn into thinking about the day-to-day life of an early rail line establishment.

The various materials that Ogoki River Guides had on file were also made available to me. From these, profiles were made of workers' incomes, duration of employment, and other characteristics of the local labour force. In addition, a most revealing part of this search was the correspondence between ORG officials and representatives of various government agencies. These letters were useful in determining local/outside differences over such things as attitudes about development and the political self-determination issue. In fact, all of the records discussed above made important contributions to my understanding of historical, economic, and political processes in Collins. They were also my primary source of statistical material, and were about the only concrete basis on which to judge the accuracy of informants' recollections.

Observation and Participation

Observation and participation should not be considered mutually exclusive sets of activities since for most purposes it is difficult to separate the two. However, I had trouble making observations in any disciplined way while participating in some activity. Participation usually meant that notes had to be hurriedly jotted down at some future time, a situation where details could be lost. Much of my participation took place either in the context of bush outings, such as fishing and hunting trips, or social gatherings in the village. My restricted use of the language was somewhat of a hinderance at parties or other large affairs, but this was less of a problem in the bush where verbal expression, for reasons of hunting and fishing success, is often kept to a minimum. Making a trip to surrounding communities, sometimes to visit but mostly to buy food or store goods not locally available, was a frequent occupation of most Collins people. These trips were usually made on a group basis, which facilitated my participation on these excursions. A person going out would frequently purchase items for those staying behind in the village, and this arrangement allowed me to participate in a wider circle of reciprocal behaviour involving the local exchange of goods and services.

Informants were not on the whole paid for their services, as an informant would usually rebuff such an attempt. Instead, I tried to do other things for them, such as typing letters or purchasing small gifts on an outside trip. Planting a garden was another of my attempts to reciprocate, as children going home from school could help themselves to a snack of potatoes, beans, or whatever else was easily reached.

Observation as a research technique was used on only limited occasions. I found that it was best employed in the work environment, where, in any event, I was not allowed to participate. On different occasions I spent most of the day perched on top of a tower overlooking the construction site of Collins's new tourist lodge at Whitewater Lake. From here I could easily count the men working at various jobs, record the time spent on different activities, and otherwise watch the overall patterns of work behaviour. I also liked to spend time in the Collins store watching the comings and goings of people and goods throughout the week. The arrival of the passenger train was another occasion where observation was used to understand the flow of activity of large groups.

Notes on various activities such as the arrival of the train or construction of a building were kept in different note books. A separate book was used to record the organization of social life, including genealogies, family histories, marriage patterns, and population data. Another book contained matters relating to economic behaviour—

income, employment, expenditures, and so on. With these notes as sources of raw data, I then made an attempt each day to organize this material into some larger argument or framework for discussion. By trying to tie the data together at an early stage I was better able to determine the direction of study and areas where more data gathering was needed. However, the most beneficial aspect of this technique was that it allowed me to follow changes in my own perception and interpretation of village affairs, which otherwise would have been oblivious to me.

The Exchange Approach

The study of exchange and gift giving by leaders in socio-political relationships has been one of the most enduring concerns of generations of anthropologists. In fact it would be entirely appropriate to suggest that a focus on exchange behaviour has been one of those rare instances in anthropology where we have had a common problem to work on for the last five or six decades. Besides organizing anthropological effort around a common theme, the exchange approach has also offered great hopes for answering some of the social sciences' oldest issues, such as: How and why do social relationships (or village, family, society, etc.) begin and end? Why do people submit to power? Are human beings social animals because of some instinct or psychological tendency, or is it simply because we choose to live the way we do? Essentially, those anthropologists working in the exchange perspective would probably begin to answer these questions with the idea that human society began when people started to realize that there were benefits to be gained by interacting with others. As time goes on a diversity of exchange patterns emerge, some involving material items (axes, salt), others being less tangible (love, prestige). These patterns become part of local customs, reproducing themselves from generation to generation, and predisposing others to do the same.

It is reasoning along these lines that has lead anthropologists to confront some important issues, such as the nature of the relationship between social structure and social action. Since this is such an important area of concern, it is not surprising that the study of exchange should play a key role in the development of the discipline, and should stimulate the efforts of some of its most productive minds, such as Boas's (1897) account of the Kwakiutl potlatch of coastal British Columbia or Malinowski's (1961 [orig. 1922]) study of the Trobriand Kula ring.

The origins of the exchange perspective in anthropology can be traced to a small group of turn-of-the-century sociologists led by Emile Durkheim. One of Durkheim's most basic ideas, which became a sort of hallmark of the French structuralist tradition, is that social phenomena could be understood as a product of collective "consciousness":

nothing collective can be produced if individual consciousnesses are not assumed; but this necessary condition is by itself insufficient. These consciousnesses must be combined in a certain way; social life results from this combination and is, consequently, explained by it. Individual minds, forming groups by mingling and fusing, give birth to a being, psychological if you will, but constituting a psychic individuality of a new sort (Durkheim 1938 [orig. 1895]: 103).

Thus, when Durkheim talks about "a psychic individuality of a new sort," he is referring to a collective awareness or group mind which is expressed in the behaviour of the individual members of the social group.

Durkheim's attempt to transcend the individual psychological level, to explain social facts as a product of collective experience, was a task to which his nephew and most distinguished student, Marcel Mauss, expended considerable effort. In his *Essai sur le don* (The Gift) Mauss produced the first systematic and comparative study of the widespread custom of gift exchange and the first understanding of its function in the organization of social order. Like Durkheim, Mauss sought to reduce a complex phenomenon to its basic underlying elements, which in Mauss's case meant taking the idea of group mind a step further than his predecessors by explaining social behaviour in terms of archetypical "collective representations." Such apparently diverse practices as the potlatch and Kula are seen by Mauss as examples of an "archaic" form of exchange characterized by a "circulation of objects side by side with the circulation of persons and rights" (Mauss 1954 [orig. 1924]: 45).

The idea that social life is understandable as expressions of the principle of reciprocity provided the basis for another influential work, *The Elementary Structures of Kinship*, by Claude Lévi-Strauss. In keeping with the heritage bequeathed by Durkheim and Mauss, Lévi-Strauss suggests that human beings have a universal psychological need for giving and receiving gifts. Furthermore, in order to understand the basic forms of reciprocity and exchange, "one must appeal to certain fundamental structures of the human mind" (Lévi-Strauss 1949: 108). In this context reciprocity is seen as the resolving mechanism between "self and others." With the resolution of this basic opposition, the individual's psychological security and the solidarity relations of the social group are enhanced.

In Britain, with the shedding of nineteenth-century evolutionism, social anthropology underwent a reconstruction on the foundations laid by Durkheim's theory of social solidarity. Durkheim's basic assumption that social systems are maintained over long periods of time in a more or less balanced state, characterized by a high degree of cohesion among its members, is a starting point for much of the "functionalist" school during the 1920s. The most important research in this early period was conducted by Bronislaw Malinowski (1961) on the economy of the Trobriand Islands.

The subject of primitive economics was of the greatest importance to Malinowski, and much of *Argonauts* is devoted to a multi-faceted system of exchange called the Kula ring. Through trading systems such as the Kula ring a society can obtain goods scarce in its own territory and dispose of goods it has in abundance. Such trade between neighbouring peoples may also be a factor crucial to their survival, thus increasing the importance of maintaining good relations. In a region such as the Trobriand Islands where no political system exists for preserving peace, an established exchange network may reduce hostilities and social tensions among the residents of adjacent island communities. Since reciprocal gift-giving and trade within the Kula area tends to equalize the distribution of goods between communities, the Kula system shares a number of characteristics with the potlatch practiced by Indian villages of the northwest Pacific coast. At a potlatch, a chief and his group give away pieces of copper, blankets, large quantities of food, and other items to their guests. Later the host chief and his group would be invited to be guests at other potlatches. The Kula and potlatch ceremonies, then, have the effect of equalizing the consumption of food and other goods not only within a village, but over a fairly widespread area. From this perspective the Kula operates in a way similar to the potlatch because they both promote the intertwining of local economies and the leveling of supply and demand. The shell ornaments of the Kula members, and the "coppers" of the potlatch chiefs, are then primarily important in an ideological sense— they serve as symbols of commensurability and co-operation.

In North America, under the influence of Franz Boas and his students, the potlatch was seen to defy analysis in terms of a rational or reasoned allocation of resources. Ruth Benedict, for example, characterized the Kwakiutl potlatch as "unabashed megalomania" (1959 [orig. 1934]: 169). From this perspective the potlatch comes to resemble a pathological disorder, or a collective mania. Even more, the potlatch appears to cast the whole Kwakiutl society in disarray, as indicated by Benedict's comment that "The whole economic system of the Northwest Coast was bent to the service of this obsession" (1959: 172). As with Mauss and Lévi-Strauss, Benedict's interpretation of an important system of exchange hardly rises above an appeal to instinctual drives and psychological states of mind.

The modern approach to redistributive systems such as the Kula and potlatch owes much to the insights provided by the field of comparative cultural ecology, such as Helen Codere's (1950) *Fighting with Property*. By concentrating on the material conditions crucial to the maintenance of social life, rather than on psychological states of mind, the Kula and potlatch are removed from the realm of the enigmatic and unknowable. It is for this reason that we find ourselves in fundamental disagreement with Robert Lowie, another of Boas' influential students, when he comments that "when a Kwakiutl in a paroxysm of vainglory confounds a social rival by destroying a canoe and breaking a copper plate valued at a thousand blankets, the motive is manifestly as far removed from the economic as it can well be" (Lowie 1920: 356). Lowie seems to have altogether missed the point that psychological factors which may motivate people to act in certain ways really have nothing to do with the question of whether such behaviour is amenable to economic analysis.

Recent Developments

The great failing of the pre-1950 exchange theorists was an aversion to placing exchange systems, such as the Kula and potlatch, in the context of political and economic relationships. Significant steps have been taken during the last two decades to present a new perspective on exchange. This new perspective recognized the materialistic conditions of human society, and the political struggles that frequently occur within it.

This brings us to the question of power, and how it affects exchange. An important attempt to deal with this problem has been made by Peter Blau (1964) in his book, *Exchange and Power in Social Life*. His purpose is to demonstrate that the nature of power can be explained in terms of the conditions and characteristics of the exchange itself. For Blau, power exists when one party is not able to immediately offer something in return for the benefits received from another. The former party may then offer a "promissory note" or lien on future services, which in effect is an acceptance of the power held by another, since they may threaten us with a withdrawal of services in order to gain compliance. This is an interesting perspective because it suggests that the emergence of power is an inevitable aspect of social life, even if certain conditions seem to favour its emergence more than others. However, despite the ingenuity of the approach, certain key problems remain. Much of Blau's analysis rests on the emergent properties of small group interaction, such as love and friendship, but there is a question about the extent to which power is created under these conditions. Do potential leaders wait in the wings biding their time

until the appropriate conditions emerge whereby they have an opportunity to secure the compliance of others? It is reasonable to suspect
that this is rarely the case and that, following Nietzsche, those with the
"will to power" create their own conditions of compliance so that less
advantaged people develop an established need for the former's
services.

This suggests that exchange theory can be most usefully applied in
situations where people have different options or alternatives that they
match up against one another and make a decision about which course
to follow. In essence, this emphasis on decision making and negotiated
transactions forms the basis for Fredrik Barth's (1966) *Models of Social
Organization*, which marks an important point of departure for anthropologists concerned with exchange theory. A linchpin of Barth's
approach is his assertion that models of kinship, politics, or economics,
for example, must be processual and "generative"—"To study form it
may be sufficient to describe it. To explain form one needs to discover
and describe the processes that generate the form" (1966: v). Generative models are formulated by "concentrating on *transaction* as the
analytic isolate in the field of social organization" (p. 5), and "one may
call transactions those sequences of interaction which are systemati-
cally governed by reciprocity" (p. 4). As a methodological note, Barth
indicates that the study of transactional behaviour should conform to
"the formal apparatus of the Theory of Games," which "serve[s] as a
prototype for a processual model of interaction" (p. 5).

This perspective is a valuable contribution to the study of exchange behaviour because it shifts attention away from the factors
which keep social arrangements the same, to the conditions which
produce new and changing forms. But there is a problem with the
"generative" approach in that it does not explain how or why people's
interests develop in the first place, aside from their participation in
some sort of social context through which benefits become available. In
other words, by focusing on how one social form "generates" another,
Barth assumes the prior existence of social relationships which become
part of his eventual explanation. Secondly, concerning the "Theory of
Games" approach, Barth would have us believe that each individual is
able to pursue his or her own interests, and adjust to the interests of
others, with as much leeway as we could expect in an ideal-type model
of the market place. In actual fact, we find that the pursuit of our
interests are modified to a large degree by the interests of more powerful people, and as such a significant source of conflict derives from the
deliberate attempts of powerful people to prevent the attainment of
goals by others. In this light, not all interests contribute equally to the
emergence of social arrangements.

At issue here is the individualistic perspective of transactional theory, and whether it is legitimate to explain social forms as the result of factors governing the actions of individuals (cf. Kapferer 1976: 13; Easton 1972: 137). There is a tendency in current transaction and exchange theory to see individuals as relatively unrestrained by their social systems, relationships, and settings. The problem is that these wider systems and relationships tend to govern, or at least direct, small-group interaction, its content, and the conditions under which it exists. An important aspect of transactional analysis, then, is the independent effect of relationship systems on individual decisions. Such an emphasis forms an integral part of Bailey's (1969) *Strategems and Spoils* in which he analyses how emerging political leaders plan tactics and negotiate with followers, and how resources are best utilized to ensure securing the "spoils" of office. This work also demonstrates that for practical purposes individual choices are never wide open, but are restricted in various ways by decisions already made beforehand and by the resources available for use. It is this line of thought that Salisbury (1977: 111-25) follows in his attempt to show how leaders try to change short-term "transactional support" into "generalized loyalty" or clientage, and thereby reduce the costs of continued negotiations with followers.

To summarize, in the post-1950 period in anthropology there has been a shift away from explanations of exchange which rely on psychological factors to those accenting the historical and environmental context in which exchange behaviour is embedded. An important concern since the time of Blau and Barth has been with the effects that available resources have on human strategies and organizations, and conversely, the effects that decisions have on the use of resources, both human and "natural." There is also concern with the individualistic, actor-oriented perspective of exchange theory which tends to see individuals as relatively unrestrained by their social systems, relationships, and settings. For this reason anthropologists need to know more about how human behaviour is related to natural and human resources, both as constraint and as a basis for action. If society is seen as a system of interaction and exchange, then anthropology would benefit from studies of change resulting from the processes and conditions of this interaction.

The goals of the present study of Collins's emergent leadership are oriented in this direction, that is, in the direction of showing how studies in exchange theory can be improved when a clearer emphasis is put on linking small group processes with wider relationships and settings. The actions of Collins's individual leaders, for example, are studied in some detail, but in the forefront of the analysis is a concern with the effects that local socio-economic relationships in Collins, and the wider governmental sphere, have on the decisions taken by such leaders. Considerable attention is also given to the way leaders' decisions are influenced by the resources available to them. In this case the term "resources" is broadly interpreted to include such things as the native work force in the Collins area, the physical setting of northern Ontario, the government funding available to the native community, as well as the skill, knowledge, and cultural traditions of the Ojibwa people themselves. The reason for making these aspects of leadership an explicit area of concern in this study is an attempt to move beyond the threshold of current exchange theory by demonstrating the important effects that wider relationships and settings have on the course of emergent leadership. In addition, the various transactions and exchanges that are initiated by Collins leaders in order to gain influence, whether they involve local people or government officials, are explicitly studied in the context of political and economic processes. In other words the concern is with the material conditions crucial to the maintenance of social life, and the political activity that emerges from a variable distribution of power, rather than with psychological states of mind. Thus, from a theoretical perspective, much of the motivation for this book stems from a conviction that constraints on leadership behaviour in the form of cultural systems, historical relationships, and ecological settings must be made an integral part of transactional theory if it is to fulfill its promise as a general guide in anthropological research.

Scope of the Study

Research in Collins began with three general problems as my focus: What factors led to the formation of this rail line community? How had it managed to remain intact after the decline of the trapping economy? Why did it have such forceful and effective leadership? A theoretical position was adopted with regard to the three problems such that Collins's continued vitality is understandable in terms of an efficient system for distributing goods and services managed by a skilled local elite. As such, a logical focus of my field work was to determine the influence of emergent leadership on economic development.

Chapter Two sketches in the historical processes which attracted northern Indians to the rail line, both as trappers looking for better terms of trade and as the beginning of a local labour force. It also presents some of the prominent aspects of Collins's contemporary social organization, such as the clustering of households within particular neighbourhoods and the role of marriage as an integrative mechanism in village life. Chapter Three, more lengthy, examines economic activity in the community. The evolution of wage work is discussed in terms of local concepts of mobilizing a labour force. It also studies the current distribution of wage incomes, the work in which people are engaged, and the importance of country food in keeping down the cost of living in the North.

In Chapter Four a more explicit focus is taken on the emergence of community leadership. The Ogoki River Guides organization is clearly shown to be the main motivator of economic change in Collins, and some of the strategies its leaders use to gain support and obtain benefits for followers are isolated. In Collins, emergent leadership and economic opportunity are interdependent factors of development. Chapter Five contains a case study of the Whitewater Lake construction project and an analysis of the problem of organizing a work force. Also included is a discussion of the role of perceptions of leadership in the work environment, and how they change in response to new conditions. In Chapter Six the salient features of economic and political change in Collins are drawn together. I raise the problem of why Collins has been successful at maintaining economic viability and local political efficacy. The answer involves two sorts of factors. "Primary" ones contribute directly to the success of projects, such as the way resources are distributed or opportunities exploited. The "secondary" factors involve the conditions favourable to the attainment of development goals, but are not determining factors in their own right, such as the ongoing process of social change in Collins or a new access to outside resources. The study concludes with some observations on the need for local initiative in economic development and for changes in government dealings with Indian communities.

CHAPTER TWO

Collins: A Non-Reserve Indian Community

Historical Background

Completion of the Canadian National Railway (CNR) in 1911 signalled the start of new beginnings for the people of northern Ontario. A multitude of new trading posts emerged almost overnight along the rail line, offering the Hudson's Bay Company its first real competition in the area since the demise of the Nor'westers a hundred years earlier. Railroad construction, Innis (1970: 363) notes, "led to a marked increase in competition where former servants of the Company deserted to join the ranks of the competitors." Independent fur traders had the advantage of inexpensive transportation costs, which meant that they could offer high fur prices coupled with low-cost food and trade goods. To give an example, customers were charged $2.55 for twenty-four pounds of flour and six pounds of rolled oats at the Collins store in 1955, while the same goods at the HBC post at Fort Hope cost $6.12 (Baldwin 1957: 79-83). It was through economic incentives such as these that much of the Albany River trade was diverted to the rail line.

The early success of line stores was also due to another important factor—escalating population growth in the Fort Hope area coincident with the establishment of the railroad (Figure 1). As population increased, trappers were pushed to the peripheral and less utilized areas of the band's territory. This process tended to isolate northern trappers from HBC influence and to increase gravitation towards independent traders. Records of the Indian Affairs Branch indicate that between 1909 and 1945 the population of Fort Hope increased by a startling 54 percent. Even more dramatic, half of this increase occurred in just a ten year period prior to 1945. After this date there is a sharp decline in Fort Hope's resident population, indicating substantial movement of persons away from the home community.

If we examine the records in more detail we find an increasingly large number of Fort Hope families residing in new locations by the early 1940s, first at the larger centres of Sioux Lookout and Pickle Lake, and later at the rail line villages of Collins and Ombabika (Table 1). Within a decade thirty-five Fort Hope families were not only trading at rail line locations, but trapping there as well (Table 2). Only a few families, about 15 percent of the Fort Hope population, were still trapping in the vicinity of the reserve by the mid-1950s. In other words, there were now more Fort Hope families trapping and trading close to the railroad than in the home area, and Collins became a major focus of this demographic shift.

FIGURE 1

Population Change for the Fort Hope Band, 1909-49

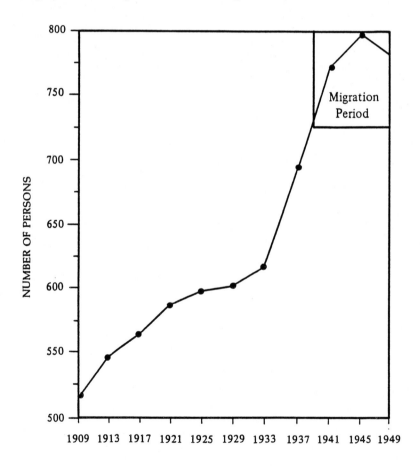

TABLE 1

Locations of Fort Hope Families Receiving Treaty Payments, 1941-45

	1941	1942	1943	1944	1945
Fort Hope	94	96	63	63	88
Lansdowne	58	45	65	64	63
Trout Lake	4	6	1	1	—
Ogoki	2	3	—	—	—
Osnaburgh	2	—	3	4	4
Pickle Lake	—	1	16	33	5
Sioux Lookout	—	2	13	24	2
Ombabika	—	1	—	—	18
Collins	—	—	—	—	13
Other[a]	1	2	4	4	4

[a] Lac Seul, Attiwapiskat and Frenchman's Head.
Source: Indian Affairs Branch records of treaty payments, 1941-45.

TABLE 2

Trapline Areas for Three Ojibwa Bands, 1954-55

Trapline Area	Fort Hope	White Sand	Nipigon House
Ombabika	9	3	—
Armstrong	—	12	—
Collins	26	3	3
Savant Lake	—	1	2
Fort Hope	29	—	—
Lansdowne	117	—	—
Pickle Lake	34	—	—

Source: Indian Affairs Branch records (1954-55), and Baldwin (1957).

The Village Today

Passengers on CNR's northern route from Quebec City through Ontario (Map 1) tend to gaze aimlessly at the green ribbon of boreal forest that streams by their window. Their trance is interrupted only occasionally by the short "whistle-stops" along the way. Slightly bewildered, they glance back and forth between their paperbacks and the rush of brown faces emerging from the bush, seemingly from

MAP 1

Northern Ontario Settlements and River Systems

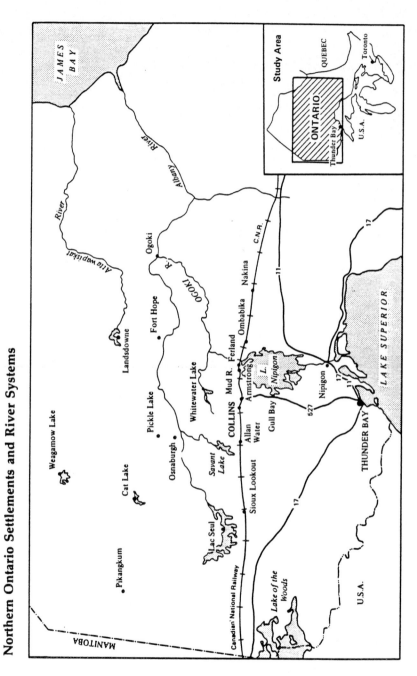

nowhere. Passengers who attempt to disembark at such places are immediately swallowed up in a whirl of frenetic activity. All about the landing dock is the din of shouting people, screeching brakes, and barking dogs. Supplies, baggage, and mail are quickly hustled aboard. Within minutes one hears only the muted rumble of diesel engines as the locomotive lumbers down the tracks.

Although the familiar sights of city life cannot be found here, a short look about reveals new points of orientation—a large clearing with trading store and one-room school, a canopy of tall jack pine, a maze of wide foot paths, log cabins scattered along a lake shore. The major part of the village is compressed between the rail line and the shore of Collins Lake (Map 2). About one-quarter of the homes are located on the north side of the tracks, and these tend to be more widely separated than those found nearer the lake. There is only one family that does not live within easy walking distance of the store; its members reside some three miles west of Collins at a place called Schultz's Trail which is a preferred fishing location. Except for the teacherage, the thirty-five houses in the village are constructed of horizontal logs and for the most part are heated by wood stoves. The Roman Catholic church has only a small following in Collins. The building itself is in desperate need of repair and services are held there only once every two or three months. The Anglican church, situated right beside the author's cabin, was destroyed in a shocking blaze just two hours before the inaugural service of a new pastor. The pastor's previous posting was in Jamaica, which probably accounts for his regrettable mistake of filling a rotted stove with kindling, lighting it, then leaving the building to visit parishioners. Another pastor was installed shortly afterwards in a beautifully crafted new building, constructed with community-donated labour and materials. In recent years the Pentecostal sect, which uses the school house for services, has virtually engulfed the community. It is too early to tell what effect the conversions will have on the people, but the general abstinence from alcohol and even tobacco are in many instances in striking contrast to the "rough-and-tumble" community familiar in my early visits a decade before.

All homes in the village are interconnected by a series of sandy paths, several of which extend past the inhabited area to nearby lakes, wood cutting sites, hunting spots, the cemetery, and gravel pit. A predominant demographic characteristic of Collins is that people's houses tend to be clustered in relatively distinct neighbourhoods. When tracing genealogies I came to learn that home clusters within neighbourhoods generally comprise people who formerly belonged to the same extended-family hunting group or winter-trapping settle-

MAP 2

Plan of the Village of Collins

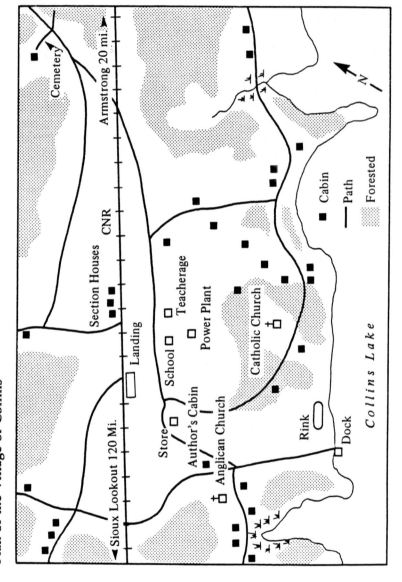

Cemetery

Armstrong 20 mi.

CNR

Section Houses

Sioux Lookout 120 Mi.

Landing

Teacherage

School

Power Plant

Store

Author's Cabin

Anglican Church

Catholic Church

Rink

Dock

Collins Lake

■ Cabin

— Path

Forested

N

ment. Accordingly, people within neighbourhoods also tend to have the same band affiliation. In broad terms members of the White Sand band occupy the east end of the village, Fort Hope people are located in a more tightly packed area around the Catholic church and store, while the Nipigon House group live in the west end near the Anglican church. A small clustering of Fort Hope families also reside on the higher, more heavily wooded north side of the rail line.

Households within these neighbourhoods are linked through ties of kinship and marriage, yet it would be incorrect to refer to them as corporate groups. Membership in the different neighbourhoods is only roughly defined, there are no overall leaders or authority structures for each neighbourhood, nor do their members regularly participate in joint economic ventures or social gatherings exclusive of other such units. Since an authority structure capable of controlling the actions of other members in the community does not exist, at least in the formal sense, social control is now largely a matter for the Eurocanadian system. Minor offenses, such as assault, theft, or property damage, are often settled by the community members themselves. Serious crimes, although rare, call for the intervention of the Ontario Provincial Police. Since the nearest OPP detachment is over twenty miles away at Armstrong, constables often arrive a day or two after the event.

In lieu of outside legal procedures, community members do make attempts to control trouble makers. Basically these attempts involve gossip and passive resistance for the most part, although physical confrontations take place from time to time. Consider the case of the sudden, unexpected arrival of a middle-aged man in Collins. In contrast to the usual festival-like atmosphere which occasions the arrival of the passenger train, everyone who witnessed this man's departure from the rail car appeared to go into a state of shock. People quickly scurried home, leaving the stranger standing alone at the landing dock. After making a few enquiries I discovered that the stranger was in fact well known to the people—a decade earlier he had shot and killed a Collins resident in the nearby village of Allenwater. The stranger had just been released from prison, and people were frightened.

After the initial alarm had subsided there was a lot of talk in the village about how to handle the situation. After supper I hurried over to see the storekeeper, John McTavish. He and his two brothers, Tom and Allen, are important people in Collins. The brothers were gathered at the house when I arrived, casually bantering about the affairs of the day. They had just begun construction of a tourist lodge at Whitewater Lake about fifty miles north of Collins and this activity was the usual focus of discussion. The arrival of the unwanted visitor was dealt with in a discussion about hiring more men. To paraphrase one leader's thoughts on the matter: "Why don't we send him to Whitewater. We can keep an eye on him there, and if I remember rightly he used to be a good worker." He then went on to espouse the virtue of rehabilitation, although no one really needed any more convincing. The stranger was eager to work, but the thirty-or-so men at the camp were troubled by all of this and refused to associate with him. Apparently the stranger found the isolation uncomfortable because he flew back from White-water in less than a week, and subsequently departed for Sioux Look-out on the next available train.

Incidents such as this bind people together while they consider their common concerns. Acts of expulsion may enhance feelings of community solidarity, but such feelings are often transitory. Kinship, contiguity, and permanence of residence, and a feeling of distinctive-ness when compared with other communities are probably more im-portant factors in promoting a sense of social cohesion among Collins people.

The Village Population

Shortly after my arrival in the village a census of the population was taken with the aid of one of the storekeeper's brothers who, especially in the initial stages of the research, acted as my translator and general tour guide. After everyone had been accounted for, and their ages checked where possible with Indian Affairs band lists, the results were compiled according to three variables—sex, year of birth, and whether or not the individual has treaty status as evidenced by the presence or absence of their name on band rolls (Figure 2). The population pyr-amid indicates that over half of the 148 residents of Collins are under twenty-one years of age, a third are between twenty-one and fifty, and the remainder are fifty years of age or over. The oldest person at eighty-seven, still spends much of his time in the bush hunting or fishing. Most other elderly residents are just as active. On one occasion while a few miles away from the village I was startled on the trail by a couple jogging along with a canoe on their shoulders; the man was eighty and his wife a spry sixty-five.

In Collins there is a near-perfect symmetry of the sexes overall (seventy-five males to seventy-three females) although unequal distri-butions exist for some age categories. Considering the small size of the total population, certain anomalies can be expected, such as the fact that males outnumber females nearly two to one in the twenty-to-forty age group. Basically there are two main causes for this disparity in the sex ratio of those in their twenties and thirties. In the first place single men who have migrated to Collins from surrounding Indian bands have not often been successful at finding a wife in the community. Secondly, local women have tended to marry men from nearby communities with greater frequency than has been the case with local men marrying women from outside. This is not entirely surprising because if we look more closely at the women who have married out we find that for the most part they have come from families with a high female-to-male ratio. In one family comprising two brothers and four sisters, three of the women married men from outside the community. In another case where the children consisted of one male and four females, three of the women eventually married out, while in another family of four daughters only one married a Collins man (the other three, while unmarried, moved to Winnipeg). As one might expect from this situation, unmarried males outnumber unmarried females by four to one for this (twenty to forty) age group.

FIGURE 2

Collins Ojibwa Population Pyramid, 1974

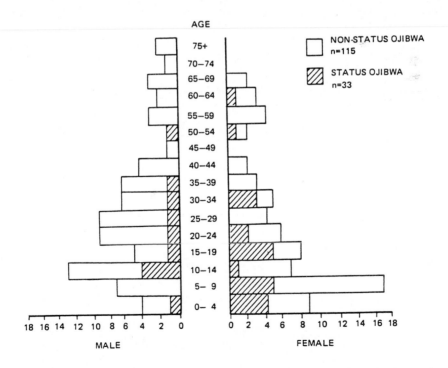

Another example of the peculiarities of small scale populations is that among the children (those under six years) of Collins the number of females is over twice that of their male counterparts. Accordingly, one can expect that within twenty years or so about a dozen women will likely move to nearby settlements, and thereby cause a reduction of thirty or forty persons in the Collins population of the year 2000.

We should also note that there is a relatively large number of widowed persons in Collins (six men and six women) which can be attributed in part to the lack of medical facilities in the area until recently, coupled with the rigours of bush life. The pyramid further indicates that a gap occurs in the number of people born in the 1920s. The major reason for this is that a serious influenza epidemic in the winter of 1908-1909 caused the death of at least eighty Fort Hope people (Skinner 1911: 118), thereby resulting in the birth of fewer children over the next two decades. But as the Collins population distribution indicates, there is considerable potential for future growth. Forty-three percent of Collins people are under sixteen years of age. For this reason we can anticipate a continuing stress on existing facilities, especially schooling and health care.

People temporarily absent from the community constitute about 10 percent of the population. Five families whose heads are CNR employees were located at various points along the rail line within a few hundred miles west of Collins. In one case the worker and his wife left their children in Collins with the husband's parents for the school year, eventually resettling in Collins when a job opening became available in the local section crew. Another young family, whose head is also a CNR employee, returns to Collins every other weekend to visit relatives. The remainder of the absentee group consists of four young women who are either working or attending school in Thunder Bay and Winnipeg.

Household Membership

Members of the same household form the most basic unit of socio-economic co-operation in the settlement. In all, there were thirty-two occupied houses in Collins, which yields an average of about four persons per dwelling. It appears that Collins has a somewhat smaller household size than that found in other Ojibwa settlements in the area (cf. Bishop 1974: 56-57). The composition of Collins's thirty-four households (in two cases dwellings were partitioned in half, with each half occupied by separate families) is summarized in Table 3. In all there is considerable variation in household composition, extending from households with only one individual to those with as many as four adult members.

TABLE 3

Composition of Collins Households, 1974-75

Household Type	Number
Individuals: male	4
female	1
Single parents with dependent children	3
Solitary couples	6
Couples with dependent children	7
Nuclear family with husband's relatives	4
Nuclear family with wife's relatives	2
Fragment nuclear family	7
Total	34

Single individual households are typically occupied by widows, migrant males from other bands, or young men without any remaining close kin in the community. In addition, there are three households comprising single adults with dependent children, and six households of solitary couples (two newly-weds and four elderly couples). Nuclear families, that is a couple with dependent children, account for seven cases and is therefore one of the most prominent household types. Just as important, with six cases, are extended families consisting of nuclear units with other relatives in residence. Four households of this variety are augmented with the husband's relatives and two with relatives of the wife. The last category of households has a varied composition consisting of the remnants of former nuclear families, and as such can be called the "fragment nuclear" type. Examples of this sort include three households with father-son combinations, and two cases of elderly couples living with unmarried adult sons.

Households in the Bush

The biggest project that Collins people have ever initiated was the construction of a million-dollar tourist lodge north of their community at Whitewater Lake. For the most part the work force was composed of Collins men, but by the middle of the first summer additional workers were also hired from the other rail line communities of Armstrong, Ferland, and Mud River. Workers and their families were flown to the construction site with the spring break-up in late May. Each family was issued a tent and allowed to choose the site for its location. This situation therefore afforded an opportunity to study continuity and change in Collins's domestic groups, and to see if group formation is affected by a switch from village to bush life.

Upon arrival each family had to make a number of immediate decisions: Who did they want to camp with? How close to the construction site should they camp? Should they camp on the mainland or on an island? It was each family's answers to these sorts of questions that led to the spacial distribution of residential units illustrated in Map 3, and to the social relationships depicted in Figure 3. The ground plan shows that tents were erected in clusters, facing eastward, most within a mile of the construction site. Several families suggested that a desire to see the early morning sun was a determining factor in their choice of sites, but for the most part, people chose a site close to the shoreline, often on a rocky projection into the lake, where there was sufficient breeze to scatter the annoying clouds of mosquitoes. In addition to the tents clustered near the construction site, two other Collins families resided on the east shore of Whitewater Lake where the men worked as guides for an Armstrong tourist operator. Another family of Collins people also worked as guides at Shapuskwia Lake, a few miles to the north.

The composition of the various tent groupings and genealogical relationships of their occupants reveal a basic pattern—camps are primarily organized along lines of kinship and place of origin. Camps 1, 2, 3, and 6 are composed of Collins people, camp 4 is from Armstrong, camp 5 from Ferland, and camp 7, the base camp, is somewhat of an amorphous group comprising Collins and Mud River residents. There are no hard and fast rules that can be applied in predicting the composition of camps, although there a number of regularities. Father/ son combinations account for three cases (camps 1, 6, and 7), brother/ brother unions in two cases (camps 2 and 4), father-in-law/son-in-law links in four cases (camps 2, 3, 4, and 7), and brother-in-law/brother-in-law ties in camp 2. It is therefore evident that a basic pattern for camp composition is for preference of common residence by males with consanguineal links. A secondary preference is residence with a family of affines, thirdly with any other relatives, and lastly, with residents of one's home community.

In order to illustrate changes in the composition of camps through time we shall examine the growth of the largest camp (2). This camp of Collins people started with the arrival of C and D along with their children in one of the initial spring-time flights to Whitewater Lake. In a later flight the family is joined by D's sister (F) and her husband (G) and brother-in-law (H). D and F's single brother (E) then moved over from the base camp. The last to join the group was C's sister (B) and her husband (A). The interesting fact about this last move was that A already had a father and brother on the site, but they were living at the base camp. Since A does not reside with his father and brother (both widowers) in Collins, this atypical case of matrilocal residence is maintained in the bush camp.

MAP 3

Plan of Whitewater Lake Summer Work Camps

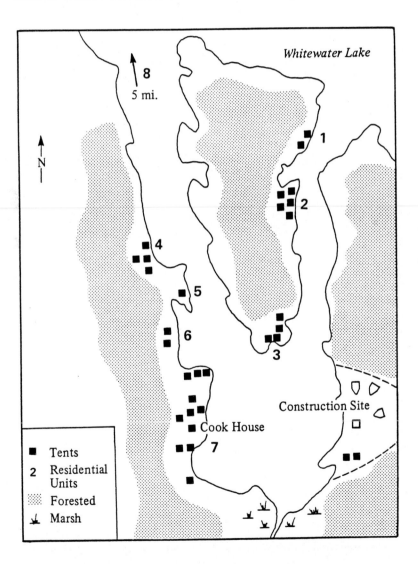

FIGURE 3

Composition of Residential Units and Genealogical Relationships in Whitewater Lake Summer Camps

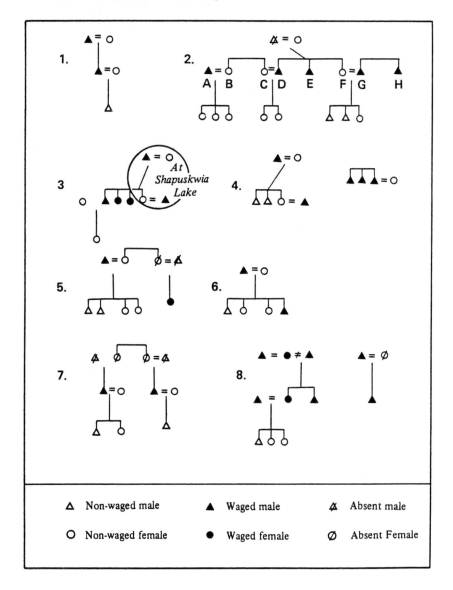

If we examine the day-to-day operation of these bush camps we find that they more closely resemble patterns found among hunting groups than is the case with village households. In Collins there are few co-operative ventures which serve to unite different households, but in the bush environment co-operative work patterns are much more prevalent. At Whitewater Lake men from the same camp were frequently seen fishing or hunting together on their off-hours, pooling the catch and distributing it among the different camp families. At the small store on the building site it was common to see one person doing the shopping for the other families in the same camp. Women look after each other's children and co-operate in cooking and camp maintenance. However, money earned on the job and purchases from the store other than food are the property of the individual and as such are not normally shared with other camp members.

In an earlier study of northern Ojibwa in the Pekangekum area Dunning noted that "The new population grouping is less bound by environmental strictures and consequently changing social norms are free to develop more uniformly along lines of a sociological form rather than an environmental control" (1959a: 108). For our purposes the question is what are these "lines of a sociological form" for the work camps at Whitewater Lake? We have already noted that camps are mainly structured along kinship ties linking male kin, but there are a number of other instances (camps 2, 3, 4, 7, and 8) where workers are linked through matrilateral and affinal kin. Since the hunting-trapping groups of a few decades earlier showed much stronger patrilineal tendencies, it is evident that a shift is occurring among Collins people to a more bilateral emphasis in group composition.

One reason for this movement from a patrilineal to a bilateral emphasis is that wage employment does not usually necessitate the solidarity of patrikin as was the case in former times. When the Ojibwa were solely hunters and trappers it was necessary that they remain in the territory that they knew best, i.e., in the territory in which they grew up. By contrast, in a wage economy there are few incentives for remaining in a particular geographical setting. Nevertheless we are still left with the question of why households in Whitewater work camps bunch together if the new wage economy does not promote social solidarity.

In order to answer this question it is necessary to realize that there are tasks facing each household at Whitewater which require a degree of co-operation different from that existing in the village. The White-water camp store supplies mainly dry goods and vegetables. It seemed uneconomic to fly meat to the bush camp when supplies of fish and game were so readily available. (Gill nets are used almost exclusively around Collins, but at Whitewater these are unnecessary since, in the right location, pickerel can be caught with nearly every cast. Moose are plentiful too; one morning two moose meandered through a camp, entangling their legs in a maze of guy ropes, but in the confusion neither animal was shot.) This means that men spend more time on subsistence activities each day at Whitewater than they do when at home in the village. When men at Whitewater were asked why they co-operate with other men in hunting and fishing their general response was that, since they had to spend so much time at the construction site, their time was limited. Time could be saved by working as a team because doing so meant greater individual returns. Women also benefit from co-operative effort, especially in the collection of firewood. More wood is consumed using an open fire than is burnt using the small stoves employed in the village, and so many women working together help maintain fire wood stocks better than each could individually. In addition, since travel between camps is virtually impossible without a boat, a larger camp means that women need not be isolated all day from contact with other people. For these reasons both men and women prefer the company of other couples in order to share in the extra tasks confronting each household in the bush environment.

Band Membership

Criteria used in the Eurocanadian categorization of native people, such as "status," "non-status," or "Métis," does not have a cultural analogue in the phenomenological world of the northern Ojibwa. An eliciting of taxonomy for "kinds of human being" in Ojibwa, e.g., "What kinds of people are there?" *denoowag bamahdeziwad uhyahwad*, leads to the discovery that the Ojibwa term for "people" *anishenabek* is also semantically equivalent to the term for "Indians" (cf. Black 1969: 176-77). The Ojibwa term *anishenabek*, then, functions both as a term for "human beings" and as a term for "Indians" when contrasted with, for example, "black people" *mukuhday weyasek*, "white people" *wahbushkeyasek*, or "Asians" *ahnebishk-ininiwek*. Furthermore, Ojibwa speakers recognize sub-classes for "Indians," such as *Ochipway* and *Maskaygo-inini* (swampy Cree), and for "whites"—*Kitchi-mokomaun* (American), *Shagunash* (Englishman), and *Uhmtegooshay* (Frenchman).

By contrast, such Eurocanadian labels as "status" and "non-status" do not form part of the Ojibwa taxonomy for "Indians," probably because these terms only have relevance in dealings with the outside world. According to people in Collins, non-status and Métis people are all considered *anishenabek* if they meet certain criteria which distinguishes them from outsiders, such as fluency in Ojibwa, "living like Indians," and more important, an individual's network of kin ties with other *anishenabek*. At any level of inclusion lower than *anishenabek*, distinctions tend to be made on the basis of kinship and band affiliation. It is necessary to indicate, however, that an Ojibwa's conception of band membership is different from that of Eurocanadians. From the government perception, band membership is based on the sole criterion of inclusion on a band list in which members can be added or excluded. For the Ojibwa at Collins, band membership is considered an extension of the kinship idiom and, accordingly, one is a member of one's band for life. When a status Ojibwa woman marries a non-status male, she will lose her band member status only in the eyes of Eurocanadians. Because of her kin ties such a woman will continue to be regarded as, for example, one of the "Fort Hope people" even after marriage. Since members of the same band are likely to have a different network of kin relations than people from other bands, the concepts of "band member" and "kin group" are inseparable by local reckoning.

The Collins population, as shown in Table 4, is composed of people from six different Ojibwa bands in northern Ontario. Fort Hope individuals form a clear majority (65%), while Nipigon House (18%) and White Sand people (12%) comprise sizeable minorities. The local population is further augmented by recent migrants from the Lake St. Joseph area (Cat Lake, Osnaburgh House, and Lac Seul). In terms of the status/non-status dichotomy, in Collins all non-status Ojibwa belong to the two largest groups (Fort Hope and Nipigon House) and non-status females outnumber non-status males by two to one.

TABLE 4

Treaty Status and Band Membership, Collins 1974-75

Band	Status		Non-status		Total	Percent
	M	F	M	F		
Fort Hope	42	36	9	9	96	65.0
Nipigon House	7	5	2	13	27	18.1
White Sand	9	9	—	—	18	12.1
Other[a]	6	1	—	—	7	4.8
Totals	115		33		148	100.0

[a] Lac Seul, Cat Lake, and Osnaburgh House.

Marriage

In an early ethnographic study of the Fort Hope Community, Alanson Skinner reported that the Ojibwa "have a considerable number of clans, which now have no importance whatever" (1911: 150). He also indicated that marriages were generally arranged by the parents of the prospective spouses, and after a presentation of gifts by the groom to the wife's father there was no further ceremony. Cross-cousin marriage, coupled with hunting group exogamy, was a prominent factor in uniting widely dispersed populations of northern Indians.

When the present study was conducted in Collins there was no evidence of cross-cousin marriage for persons under the age of forty, nor was clan or totem membership recognized. Each individual today is largely responsible for selecting his or her own marriage partner, although parents are often consulted and their approval sought. People still marry outside their (former) hunting groups but, since there are now many unrelated people brought together in the new community and migrations have tended to remove people from proximity to their cross-cousins, marriages are generally endogamous within the village.

One factor which figures prominently in the social organization of the Collins settlement is the significant difference between marriage patterns of dominant and minor groups (Table 5). People of the Fort Hope band show an over-riding preference for marriage partners from among members of their own group. Nearly three-quarters of Fort Hope marriages for which I have fairly complete genealogical information are endogamous within this dominant grooup. Nipigon House and White Sand marriages, however, are in sharp contrast to the Fort Hope pattern. Members of these smaller groups exhibit complete exogamy in their choice of marriage partners. As examples, there is the case of a Nipigon House father and his two sons who all married Fort Hope women. Similarly, a White Sand man along with his son and nephew all opted for marriage with women of the Fort Hope band. Reciprocally, this White Sand man's two daughters married related Fort Hope men.

TABLE 5

The Collins Marriage Pattern

		Marries woman			
		Fort Hope	Nipigon	White Sand	Other
	Fort Hope	16	3	2	1
Man	Nipigon	4	—	—	—
	White Sand	3	1	—	—
	Other[a]	2	1	1	—

[a] Lac Seul, Cat Lake, and Osnaburgh House.

Two reasons can be suggested to account for this marriage pattern. First, the selection of marriageable partners from among small group members is restricted by a relatively small number of potential choices in the community, although there are numerous White Sand and Nipigon House people in other nearby settlements. Alternatively, members of the smaller groups have opted to strengthen links with members of the Fort Hope group—the locus of power, influence, and its local distribution—in order to participate in a greater share of economic and political benefits available in the community. This is evidenced by the fact that I have recorded only three cases of inter-marriage between members of minor groups. By choosing the "right" spouse people can extend their circle of kindred, and thereby develop wider patterns of co-operative interaction and support.

Power and Authority

The village of Collins illustrates the heterogeneous character of many northern Indian settlements. A fur trading post provided the initial attraction for relatively large trapping-based families who lived separately from other such units scattered along the lake shore. With the coming of autumn this loosely organized community fragmented with the dispersal of families travelling back to their hunting grounds. Some of these hunting territories were as far away as the Lansdowne area on the Attawapiskat River, while others were scattered between the Albany River and Lake Nipigon. In other words, the groups congregating at Collins Lake during the summer months would have little if any contact with each other for a good part of the year. With the establishment of the Indian Affairs school in 1960 the emergence of a less transient community was taking place. Fur prices began to fall sharply in the early 1960s and the fur trader became the dispenser of increasingly larger welfare vouchers. People began to shift away from life in tents to the construction of more permanent log cabins, and the emerging settlement at Collins began to take shape.

The village today is still characterized by certain demographic, religious, and social divisions: the Fort Hope group is the numerically dominant band and occupies a central location in the village, while people affiliated with the Nipigon House and White Sand bands live on the eastern and western peripheries of the settlement; religious affiliation divides the people into Anglican and Catholic blocs; the smaller bands exemplify an exogamous marriage pattern while the larger Fort Hope is essentially an endogamous group; and, not the least important, there is a division of band members into status and non-status categories.

For the purposes of this study an important question has to do with the relative significance of these divisions in the socio-political process of the village. This question is all the more important because

the directors of ORG and their principal foremen are all members of the
dominant Fort Hope band. In addition, there are extensive bonds of
kinship and marriage which tie the members of this group into a more
cohesive unit. Such a discussion will provide an opportunity to approach subjects concerning a monopolization of power by the members of one band, and more specifically by a single family, and the
nature of the power accorded to ORG and the Fort Hope group by the
members of smaller, less influential bands.

Historically, leadership among the Ojibwa and Cree was not
rigidly formalized. This is partly understandable in terms of a rugged,
densely forested landscape which supported one of the lowest population densities found anywhere on the globe. In this situation how was
control implemented? There are, theoretically, a variety of means to
maintain control over others, but for the most part among the Ojibwa
this meant a single individual in command of a group of people, such
as would comprise the extended family, hunting group, band, and, in
recent times, the community. The individual's authority in this case is
based upon kinship, economic, or religious sanctions. Physical force
was employed only in rare circumstances. Gossip was, and still is, an
important mechanism of social control but is not a necessary leadership
skill. For the Ojibwa, leadership involved a constellation of features
which defined the "leader" role. These features or characteristics consist of a leader's responsibilities and degree of power and authority.

The hunting group, composed usually of several closely related
nuclear families, was most often under the authority of the eldest male
member. He was responsible for directing the movements of the group
throughout their hunting territory, for guiding religious ceremonies,
and for distributing food among group members. In general, leaders,
whether male or female, worked hard and thereby had a surplus to
distribute, attaining power through ability and personal influence. The
leadership role was not acquired through an election to office but
through the tacit consent of the people. As the fur trade grew in
importance so did the Indian leader's ability to speak well and to act as
an intermediary or arbitor between the group and the European. We
might conclude that under these conditions a leader maintained power
more by ingenuity and personal prowess than by any rigidly defined
criteria for the role holder. The very nature of this sort of leadership
suggests that the sanctions which maintained the leader's role were
probably largely based on public opinion. The picture is one where the
hunting-group elders possessed the actual power and comprised a
kind of council which arrived at general agreements. It was the group
"leader" who had the ability to put these agreements and understanding into words.

The creation of trading posts provided a new focus for the Indians' summer gatherings, although there is no evidence that bands coming together at one post were not able to maintain their individuality. Overall, the fur trade provided new conditions or opportunities for genuine leaders to arise. One such individual was the boss in charge of the fur and supply brigades. These men had considerable power over those individuals settled at the trading posts because they could command obedience through economic sanctions, especially since they were backed by the traders. A related leadership role involved the "trading captains" (Morantz 1982) who negotiated with Europeans for the hunting group as a whole. The red captain's coat and medals bolstered the leader's position, but in later years this trading role collapsed as trappers themselves began to trade directly with company officials. There is evidence (Rogers 1965: 272) that the emergence of such leaders seems to be based on acculturative factors which were dependent upon the degree of contact. Such leaders were able to secure power from several sources. They were of mixed ancestry in many cases, a fact partly explaining their positions. With one European parent the potential leader would receive training allowing him to deal effectively with white traders and other outsiders. They may also have internalized a desire to get ahead or succeed in the European sense.

Leadership in Collins would appear to be an extension of this pattern. Collins's main leaders, the McTavish brothers, are the sons of a white fur trader and his Indian wife. They are clearly Ojibwa both ascriptively and in terms of their behaviour, yet Eurocanadian enough to move successfully in the larger sphere in which their community is encapsulated. The Collins leadership, in particular the McTavish triumvirate with their urban contacts and training, have used governmental sources such as the Department of Regional Economic Expansion (DREE), Agricultural Rehabilitation and Development Agency (ARDA), and the outside political and economic world in general as resources—resources which they, in contrast to the average Collins resident, know how to tap and utilize (Hedican 1982: 27-29). In part, Collins leaders succeeded because they had the necessary rewards to provide to their followers. Moreover, the material and social capital bequeathed to the McTavish brothers by their father can also be seen as a central factor in the development of ORG. It is doubtful whether ORG would have emerged at all had there been no store in Collins.

The argument here is that leadership in Collins, centred on ORG, is not in contradiction with the traditional Ojibwa political system which was to accord authority to individuals with the most experience and expertise. In the traditional pattern leadership was based on hunting and trapping skills, on maturity, wisdom, and guidance. These latter characteristics are still important, but today it is more crucial to bring home money and employment than meat and furs. Like the past, leadership today still has to be validated above all by performance. The leader capable of delivering the goods creates, in turn, a confidence or faith among followers which serves to legitimize the leader's performance. The view of Collins leaders, in particular the McTavish brothers, is that ORG has earned the right to represent the community, in the absence of elections and formal votes, because ORG has been successful at delivering jobs and other benefits. Experience and organizational skills are abilities congruent with traditional leadership concepts and, from ORG's position, validate its authority in the local affairs of Collins. Rogers's (1965: 279) comment that today "community leadership, whether formal or informal, is weakly developed among the Indians of the Eastern Subarctic" probably derives more from the fact that the chief is no longer the distributor of goods to his people than for any other reason. The idea in this study is that in Collins its leaders have managed to maintain a principal role in the local distribution of goods and services. Such a locally controlled distribution network lends credibility to village leaders, and further, provides the organizational basis through which power and authority can be extended and consolidated. Rogers's reason for the situation he outlines above is that "with a breakdown in the native culture, the people have not established new objectives or clearcut goals which would promote the development of strong leadership roles" (1965: 280). Collins is therefore an example of a northern Indian community going against the grain, so to speak, with its new objectives and strong leaders.

Now, returning to the initial problem posed at the start of this section concerning the relative importance of demographic and social divisions in the political process, as far as I can judge these divisions do not threaten the present leadership pattern as long as two conditions prevail—these divisions must not prevent people from deriving benefits, and second, they must not provide a basis for the organization of factions opposed to the current leadership practice. During the course of field work I could see almost no evidence that either of these situations was likely to emerge. For example, the status/non-status division usually has little relevance for life in Collins because it is not a reserve, and therefore status Indians do not derive special benefit from living in this settlement. However, there was one situation that had the potential to divide people along status lines, but the McTavish brothers intervened to mollify the problem. The difficulty arose when the Indian Affairs school became overcrowded and the district school board sent letters to parents indicating that only status Indian children would be allowed to attend. The McTavish brothers, whose own non-status children were also involved, informed the school board that the Collins school would remain closed until a solution could be found that would allow all children, whether status or non-status, to attend. A temporary solution was worked out by changing part of the store into a classroom. (This situation was thought to be so serious that by the end of the 1970s Collins people built their own school, formed a local school board, and now hire and fire their own teachers. They also aligned themselves with a provincial agency, the Ontario Ministry of Education, and largely terminated their association with the Indian Affairs Branch whose officials were thought to be untrustworthy.) Thus, a situation like the school crisis has the potential for divisive results among Collins people, but since the McTavish brothers were willing to intervene on behalf of the small, non-status group, these latter people felt that the current leaders were protecting their interests, as well as the interests of the community as a whole. This is a key point. As long as Collins leaders are thought to be concerned with the community at large, as opposed to the interests of a more specific group, people are willing to give them support.

In the area of job selection, for example, every opportunity was given to the White Sand and Nipigon House people to work on ORG projects, although they did not usually perform supervisory functions. Water wells were located in various parts of the village so that members of all groups would have access to uncontaminated water. The Collins marriage pattern itself seems to indicate a willingness on the part of the smaller groups to develop long-term associations with members of the larger Fort Hope group. The fact that the McTavish brothers are of mixed ancestry is probably also an important consideration. Their skills and experience satisfy external agencies. Perhaps too, on the inside, their high status comes from being quasi-outsiders. This would mean that there would be less temptation to identify the McTavish brothers with any one particular interest group in the community. The brothers, unlike most other people, cannot be easily slotted into one particular category or another: they are part of the Fort Hope group, but are legally not members of this band; both the Catholic and Anglican ministers are fed and housed by the brothers who try not to show favouritism towards either denomination, even to the point of seldom attending the services of either group; they look like white men but they speak and live like Indians. It is these various factors that make it difficult for would-be opponents to make a case that the brothers are motivated by interests favouring one group over the interests of others. It is perhaps also necessary to keep in mind that while the McTavish brothers are members of the Fort Hope "group," in no way does this mean that Fort Hopers have a monopoly on local power. The reason for this is that even though the McTavish brothers regard Fort Hope as their "home"—i.e., the place where they were born—and have many relatives in the band, they do not properly regard themselves as the leaders of the Fort Hope people residing in Collins. In any event the brothers have almost no close relatives actually living in Collins, which means fewer people using kinship as a leverage for increased favours. Their view is more of a village-wide representation where the various labels and divisions are down-played in favour of a more united approach. More importantly, they believe that government funding agencies are favourably disposed to communities that are solidly behind their leaders' initiatives.

In considering the question of local power and authority in Collins an historical point is also relevant in that the McTavish brothers did not actually monopolize existing power relationships. Before it was centralized in the form of ORG, there was practically no "formal power structure" in the community. In effect the brothers forged new power relationships, building on those bequeathed to them by their father, the fur trader and store owner. With a large unemployed population pushing from below, and various government funding agencies dangling cash from above, it is possible to see ORG as developing a momentum all its own. If, as Dunning notes for the village of Pekangekum, "in Ojibwa society . . . there is an extremely limited set of mechanisms for setting up extra-familiar relations, and hence for integration of the band or society as a whole" (1959a: 156) then the "mechanisms" initiated by ORG should be of interest in themselves. In fact, Dunning goes on to argue that "the role of gift-giving" should be examined "as the only institutional means for integrating and maintaining relationships outside the sibling group and the range of patrilateral kinsmen" (1959a: 156). ORG is like an elaborate gift-giving machine, inspired along traditional sentiments and ideals, but geared to current economic realities.

CHAPTER THREE

Economic Incorporation and Exchange

One summer day in 1534 about fifty Micmac Indians stood on the shore of Chaleur Bay in the Gulf of St. Lawrence beckoning Jacques Cartier and his men to disembark. The Indians "made frequent signs to us to come on shore, holding up to us some furs on sticks." A short time later "the two parties traded together. . . . They bartered all they had to such an extent that all went back naked without anything on them; and they made signs to us that they would return on the morrow with more furs" (Biggar 1924: 49). This may not have been the most important day in Canadian history, but there is no doubt that the development of the early fur trade would profoundly influence the economic and political growth of the nation. The fur trade also had profound effects on Indian people who over large regions began to abandon their autonomous subsistence-based life for one involving hunting and trapping for exchange purposes, thus moving into a dependency relation with Europeans.

There was much more, however, to the trade in furs than the large scale commercial expansion of European civilization. When the position of the Indian is considered, a picture of the trade emerges where trade is linked with cordiality and peaceful intentions, or in some cases as military allies. Sagard refers to a meeting of the Hurons "where I was entreated that the traders of the Company should be kindly disposed to the captains of the trade, that they should be given necessary articles of merchandise at a reasonable price and that on their side they would exchange very good furs" (Sagard 1936 [orig. 1865]: 238, quoted in Innis 1970: 17). Champlain was frequently made the object of requests not only for material goods but for assistance in quelling intertribal conflicts, since trade and peace were seen as invariably connected. In 1615 "they hoped that we would furnish them some of our number to assist them in their wars against our enemies, representing to us that they would with difficulty come to us if we should not assist them; for the Iroquois, they said, their old enemies, were always on the road obstructing their passage" (Champlain 1907: 276). When French traders tried to dissociate the profit-taking aspect of trade from the ceremonial, the Indians became mistrustful of European intentions. Such was the case when Sagard wrote that the Hurons "expostulated against the methods of our merchants in completing the trade in an hour" (Sagard 1936: 130, quoted in Innis 1970: 21).

The problem of keeping trade routes open meant that the French were obligated to form alliances with the hunting Indians against the Iroquois. Champlain was therefore engaged to help in fighting their battles, a situation described in the *Jesuit Relations* of 1611 as follows:

The remaining four tribes [Algonquins, Montagnais, Souriquois, and Etheminqui] appear already to be united in firm friendship and intimacy with them. They stay over night with us; we rove about with them and hunt with them and live among them without arms and without fear; and as has thus far appeared, without danger. This intimacy arose partly from association while fishing for Cod ... and partly from trading in furs (Thwaites 1896-1901, 2: 71).

Anthropological writings on economic exchange, especially on gift-giving by leaders in socio-political relationships, have been fairly extensive. As discussed earlier, the Kula and potlatch are widely known examples, although perhaps not the best understood. If, as noted for New Guinea exchange systems, "trade means peace ... [and] the network of exchange at a given time thus indicates inter-tribal political relations as well as the complementarity of their various economies" (Godelier 1971: 63), then we need to know more about the historical processes by which exchange relations are transformed over time. This task would be facilitated by a concern with changes which have marked Indian/European relations in the area of economic exchange, and by a focus on processes leading to the economic incorporation of Indian life into a wider system of dependency relations with whites. Accordingly, our purpose now is to examine three relatively diverse, but interconnected, periods or stages in the changing relationship between European trader and Indian trapper in northern areas.

The initial period is one of "ceremonial exchange" in which traders are heavily dependent upon the services and goods of the native population, in some instances for their very survival. The second period is of a more direct commercial or commodity exchange—traders are better able to provide their own provisions, and the practice of wage labour is introduced, although with mixed results. The period of "non-reciprocal exchange" follows in such a way that traders assume an ascendancy position in Indian/white relations. Some Indians characterize this new relationship as a form of slavery because of the Europeans' implicit concept of rank difference based on non-reciprocal obligations and asymmetrical role relationships. Using this discussion as a base line for studying change, we then proceed to a focus on the contemporary aspects of the Collins economy, discussing such things as local attitudes towards work, and the characteristics of the income distribution and consumption patterns of village residents.

Ceremonial Exchange

The history of Indian/European relations in northern Canada extends back nearly five centuries and is interwoven with the rise of western countries as commercial powers in the world. From the early exchanges between French fishermen and Algonkians on the St. Lawrence, contact with Europeans was channeled through a relatively small number of agents representing the institutions of trade and church. In this early period Europeans were heavily dependent upon the native population, primarily for food and knowledge about northern survival, and this need for native services was a basic factor conditioning initial native/white interaction.

When whites attempted to hire Indians to perform these services, however, they encountered a puzzling resistence. The first traders soon came to realize that Indian conceptions of work were virtually inseparable from their conceptions of trade. For example, when Alexander Henry was attempting to forge new trade routes to the Northwest in the 1700s he encountered a band of Ojibwa near Lake of the Woods. Henry secured a hundred bushels of wild rice and claimed that his journey to western Canada would have been impossible without the country food procured by Indians. Trading in Henry's time was characterized by formal speeches and "ceremonious presents":

On the thirteenth we reached the Lake of the Woods, or Lake des Iles, at the entrance of which we obtained a further supply of fish. From this village we received ceremonious presents. The mode with the Indians is, first to collect all the provisions they can spare, and place them in a heap; after which they send for the trader, and address him in a formal speech. They tell him that the Indians are happy in seeing him return to their country; that they have been long in expectation of his arrival; that their wives have deprived themselves of their provisions in order to afford him a supply.... The present, in return, consisted in one keg of gunpowder of sixty pounds weight; a bag of shot, and another of powder, of eighty pounds each; a few smaller articles, and a keg of rum (Henry 1969 [orig. 1809]: 241-42).

This exchange of "presents" was an important socio-political institution among northern Indians because it served to reaffirm friendship and goodwill. This feature of intertribal trade, in turn, solidified alliances among the many disparate and autonomous extended family groups across northern areas. Another factor encouraging the practice was that gift-giving by a leader to other group members maintained the leader's credibility because of the value placed on generosity. Should a leader refuse to engage in such redistribution practices he would likely become the butt of ridicule. As such, in order for the fur trader to become successful he had to adopt the appropriate cultural norm of the native population, and this was accomplished by status gains through reciprocal gift exchange and displays of generosity. In later years this situation was to change in various ways, mainly to the trader's advantage.

The first complications arose over traders' manipulation of native trading relationships. In order to keep accounting records of their barter trade, the Hudson's Bay Company established the Made Beaver (MB)—the value of one prime beaver skin—as the standard unit of valuation for all furs, country food, trade goods, and even work performed at the post. One problem with this system was that trade goods were assigned values according to the Hudson's Bay Company's *official standard of trade*, while the value of furs was reckoned according to the *comparative standard of trade*. Inflation in the cost of trade goods from Europe forced traders to find some way of adjusting local trade values to suit variations in European market conditions. Understandably, Indians were reluctant to switch from a standard rate to an upwardly changing one, so the trader's solution was to incorporate a *double standard* in trading negotiations such that trappers received short measures, or were made to trade more skins for less merchandise (Ray 1974: 61-65).

There is no evidence to indicate whether the country food that the trader received from the Indians was also placed on a sliding exchange rate, but it can be expected that the trader would cling to a standard rate when it was to his advantage. The fact that the trader remained dependent upon Indian services and goods for most of the eighteenth century must have been a particular source of concern for him. Besides meat and fish, a trader required hides for clothing, sturgeon oil for lamps, fat for candles, goose quills for pens, feathers for mattresses, birch bark, sleds, snowshoes, canoes, and so on. So severe was this dependency that in some districts the traders would send off harried notes to headquarters every winter indicating that he and his men were in the last throws of starvation. In 1792 the factor at Osnaburgh House routinely jotted in his journal "sett [*sic*] of all the Indians to hunt more Provisions or else we must starve." Four years later the situation had not grown much better for the new factor, John Best, when he filed this report: "If Inds. does not bring us Venison God knows what one are to do" (in Bishop 1974: 231).

Such was the plight of many inland posts that Indians soon found it more profitable to hunt country food than to trap furs. The Assiniboine, once forest dwellers of northwestern Ontario and northern Manitoba, had given up trapping altogether by 1780, the year that they made their last canoe trip to Fort Albany on the James Bay coast. After moving onto the Plains the Assiniboine became a main producer of dried buffalo meat, which was consumed in prodigious quantities by residents of northern trading posts (Ray 1974: 131-33). But some Indians, mainly Cree and Ojibwa, moved closer to the post as more opportunities for earning cash (actually, HBC tokens) became available—cutting ice and firewood, guiding, and transporting supplies on the York boats. Compared with hunting, though, wages were not high for these occupations. For the arduous eight-hundred-mile supply run from Fort Albany to Osnaburgh six Indians received a total of 60 MB, the equivalent of two moose or one large canoe (Bishop 1974: 234). Some less fortunate posts offered less reimbursement, the traders were left to fend for themselves, and the post was evacuated.

Commodity Exchange

By the middle of the 1800s traders were coping much better than they had in previous decades. The more problematic posts were abandoned, potato gardens were now extensively cultivated, and posts were installed at the best fisheries. Traders also became proficient at fashioning their own bush tackle, all of which were instrumental in reducing dependency on the native population. This did not mean that trading posts no longer required Indian services, only that traders' requirements became more specialized than in earlier periods. The greatest labour demand was still for workers on the supply boats, although post journals frequently indicate Indians' disdain for this job. Indians would only undertake such trips under desperate circumstances, such as when they were destitute or starving.

One post manager in 1847 commented on this situation by comparing the different responses to wage work between the Cree on the James Bay coast and the Ojibwa of the interior forests. The Cree, Charles Mackenzie noted, "are kept as Summer Labourers—fed and paid as labourers—Nay they offer their Services—while the inland Indians—can hardly be got for a summer trip. They will tell plainly—'We are poor 'tis true but we shall not be Slaves'" (in Bishop 1974: 141). One reason for this differential response to wage work among northern Indians could be that the inland Ojibwa had access to more productive fishing areas in summer than the coastal Cree. If this were the case then the Cree would be more likely to augment subsistence production with goods earned through waged work at the trading post than would be the case with interior Indians. This situation suggests that if the value of Indians' subsistence production fell below their earnings through working at the post, then either the trader would have to pay more, or be forced to hunt and fish for himself. In McKenzie's journal account he complains that the Indians he hired to work on the boats to Albany quit after only eight days since, "they had not *enough to eat* which indeed has ever been a complaint on this River" (Bishop 1974: 114). He later remarked: "True I hired an Indian to assist the only one I could get to become a Slave—(in their thinking) during the Summer—I got him because he is naked but when he and his family are clothed—'tis most foremible he may take 'a French lieve'" (Bishop 1974: 115).

Throughout most of the nineteenth century the major source of employment, in addition to trapping, still remained supply freighting, but after 1890 the route to Fort Albany was abandoned. The completion of the Canadian Pacific Railway in 1880, and the Canadian National Railway in 1910, offered a closer supply depot for interior posts. Osnaburgh House, for example, employed thirty or more men in this occupation each summer, for which each received 16 MB (about $7.50) in trade goods for each round trip to the rail line.

Non-Reciprocal Exchange

Comparative research on economic exchange (i.e. Sahlins, 1965) suggests that northern Indians, from their point of view, were not "working" for the trader as such, but considered themselves donors—giving the trader gifts of food with the expectation that he would reciprocate with an equivalent amount at some future time. Trade goods received from the trader would therefore be considered as a holder or lien, but not as a discharge of debt. As indicated above, non-reciprocal labour was viewed by Indians as a form of slavery, since the worker was never in a position to hold obligations of the boss. In other words, since non-reciprocal exchange was not based on a mutually contingent relationship, one party (the worker) was always obliged to comply with the demands of another (the donor). When Indians characterized their work situation as slavery, in essence they were objecting to Europeans' implicit concept of rank difference based on a system of non-reciprocal obligations.

The point here is not that all exchange between Indians and Europeans had to be of equal value or kind. Actually the word "bartering" implies that an exchange is unequal in some respects, but since the goal is to maximize returns each party thinks that the asymmetry is in its own favour. What is important is that the exchange retains an element of reciprocity, and that there is an exchange of goods or services valued by both sides. In cases when an exchange is valued more by one party than another, one can expect the emergence of asymmetrical role relationships. This process can be seen from the fact that leaders, called *okima* in Ojibwa or *auchimau* in Cree, did exist in northern hunting societies. As a rule these leaders contributed substantially more material goods (such as meat and skins), or nonmaterial benefits (protection and religious knowledge) to their group than did fellow band members. But in this case the leader/follower relationship was still reciprocal in the sense that while a leader's services flowed downwards to followers, respect, support, and other intangibles flowed upwards to the leader.

Consistent with this situation is the idea that followers were equivalent to adopted workers of the leader's "family." While northern Indians would not become a trader's slave, some would become semi-permanent residents of the trading post, known as "homeguard" Indians, who performed odd tasks about the post. In return the trader provided food, gifts, and sometimes clothing and housing for workers and their families. It was during this period (c. 1800-1940) that the Ojibwa word for "leader" or "boss" (*okima*) came to be applied to the post manager (Rogers 1965: 271), while the Indian leader became known as *okima·hka·n* or "chief-like" (Ellis 1960: 1). Thus, from the Indian viewpoint the European had now become a recognized authority—one accustomed to giving orders and being obeyed. Although the trader's authority revolved primarily about economic affairs, instances are recorded (Lips 1947: 483) where Indians did turn to the trader regarding social or personal matters as well. In all, the trader had gone from an obsequious irritant to an overall patron in the northern Indian community. It was not until the fur trade's decline in the 1950s that the trader began to lose his local influence.

Concepts of Labour Mobilization

Despite the pervasiveness of wage labour today, historical sources indicate that for northern Ojibwa the labour for money exchange was not considered a satisfactory arrangement. Buying labour was viewed in the same light as buying people. Indians who worked for money were "slaves" by local reckoning because in these instances there no longer existed a system of reciprocal exchange. Indians were no longer partners in joint ventures, that is joint labour exchanges, because Europeans insisted upon a system of non-reciprocal labour with its implicit superiority (boss)/inferiority (worker) dichotomy.

Yet, despite the two hundred or so years that northern Indians have worked for wages, goods, services, or other benefits, it is still possible to reconstruct some aspects of traditional thinking regarding

the mobilization of labour from an analysis of contemporary behaviour. In Collins, the idea that one "hires someone to do something"
is not indigenously recognized as a work-concept. A task is accomplished, not by "hiring someone," but by exchanging your future
labour for someone's immediate services. The second major form of
labour mobilization does not involve an exchange of labour as such,
but involves an exchange of goods and/or services in return for "professional" knowledge or skill.

For the most part the daily run of household activities can be
accomplished by members of the immediate household, yet there are
times when every household requires extra help for short periods of
time. A common instance occurs when a household has the good
fortune of killing a number of moose or other large animals at the same
time. Extra labour is required immediately in order to avoid spoilage of
the meat by the elements or predators. Help in butchering and transporting meat and skins to the village is exchanged for either a small
portion of the kill plus a promise of future help with a similar endeavour, or a larger portion, such as a front or rear quarter, with no
promise of future aid. This help/meat continuum is some indication of
a degree of elasticity in local labour demand. When demands on the
indigenous labour market are high, such as during peak subsistence
periods, a family may forego a labour/meat exchange altogether and
simply pull up stakes and move to the kill site, remaining there until
the meat is consumed or dried and the hides fleshed.

House raising is another activity involving a reciprocal labour
exchange. Although it is possible for one man to do the entire job
himself, providing that the logs used are small enough, there are
phases in house construction where most men attempt to secure extra
labour. This is especially true for the roofing stage when rain could
damage interior surfaces. It is also desirable to have extra help for some
carpentry work and the arduous task of hauling logs from the bush. In
most instances a man cuts, peels, and stacks logs in the bush by himself
as a part-time activity. Most work dealing with the actual construction
of the house usually involves other kinsmen, so that the principle of
labour repayment is likely to entail an informal labour "mortgage"—a
promise of future help, plus a meal *cum* party when the heavy work is
complete.

Another type of labour mobilization involves a form of temporary
guardianship in exchange for help around the household. A case of
this nature involves a teenage girl who was having problems while
living at the home of her grandparents. She subsequently took up
residence with a family of non-relatives (she had no other relations in
the village) who, since the death of the family's mother, were short of
female help. For several months the teenage girl looked after the

younger children and performed household chores in return for food and lodging.

For the most part rates of exchange for household-related services are less concrete than in other cases because household services usually involve relatives or friends who would consider it a breach of etiquette to insist on too strict a schedule of repayment for goods or services. However, in certain cases, such as those requiring specialized skills, there exist more concrete notions of labour repayment. In these cases it is not extra or supplementary labour that is needed, it is a demand for people considered specialists in certain areas. Native healers are a prime example of this area of labour mobilization. The two most revered specialists of this nature are old men who have built up large followings and who are well known throughout most of northern Ontario. But one must bear in mind when calculating rates of labour payment that patients will often travel hundreds of miles to visit these men and, as such, one must include the "hidden" costs of transportation, food, and lodging.

For members of communities north of the CNR the bush plane is the usual mode of transportation over long distances, especially in the case of emergencies. Such was the case when an elderly Fort Hope woman, with other relatives along for support, flew out to Nakina, then motored on to Long Lac to seek the services of Kitchi David. The old woman had complained of chest pains and headaches, symptoms which Eurocanadian doctors had little success in treating. Kitchi David treated the woman with a jar of herbal remedies in conjunction with an elaborate, twenty-foot-long, stethoscope-like device. He then concluded his treatment with the same prescription for everyone who visits him—in order for his remedy to be effective, he tells the patient, one must refrain from taking alcoholic beverages for a period of one year.

A middle-aged Collins man subsequently sought treatment from the same native doctor. In this case the patient had suffered from hallucinations (mostly about seeing snakes in the graveyard, which he considered a bad omen), and had spent time in the Thunder Bay Psychiatric Hospital because of them. The Collins man admitted that he did not discuss his problem with the Thunder Bay doctors because he could not find a way to express his suffering in terms understandable to Eurocanadians. When he returned from Thunder Bay the man went to visit the Long Lac specialist who managed to cure him, as he called it, of his "craziness." For the Collins man the charge for this specialized treatment was one new rifle, which is symbolic of subsistence activities supportive of native life styles and expertise.

Other specialists found in Collins include carpenters, small-motor mechanics, and fishermen. Payment for these services are varied. The carpenter may request help on another project, the mechanic might want the use of one's boat and motor, while fishermen charge about $5 a piece for their lake trout. We now proceed to a specific discussion of the Collins labour force outlining its composition and other characteristics.

The Collins Labour Force

As with many northern communities, the basic work activities for Collins people have until recently centred about subsistence hunting-trapping-gathering, coupled with the production of domestic handicrafts. The first opportunities for wage employment in the area, aside from trading post work, began with the construction of the CNR just after the turn of the century. But after the construction stage, which lasted for only a few years, full-time maintenance jobs generally went to outsiders. Over the last fifteen or twenty years, though, many outside workers have transferred to sections closer to the larger urban centres, and Indian people have generally filled these vacancies. Aside from railway work, the trading post in Collins employed casual workers to cut firewood, to maintain and store fish in the ice-house, and to transfer furs and supplies to and from the rail line. Two men in the 1930s worked in a small chrome mine twenty miles south of Collins, which closed during the war years when workers joined the armed forces. Both men, who were in their teens at the time, said that they were the only Indian workers, and described how they were given the "dirtiest" and most dangerous jobs around the mining camp.

The spasmodic nature of production and wage work cycles is illustrated by the following description of economic trends in Collins during the 1950s:

The trading-store owner bought a thousand dollars worth of fish from four families in 1954, no fish in 1955. Blueberries bring from $1.50 to $2.00 a basket, and the amount taken varies greatly from year to year. Ten guides were employed in 1954, six in 1955, at ten dollars a day, for about ten days each. The lumber mill at Fee Spur employed twenty in 1954, but only two in 1955 (Baldwin 1957: 92).

By the 1970s railway maintenance and activities related to the construction of the tourist lodge at Whitewater Lake account for virtually all of the full-time employment in Collins. Railway work also accounts for most of the geographic mobility in the local labour force, while the Whitewater project has spawned additional economic activities, such as the establishment of a retail outlet at the construction site and a van line to haul supplies from Thunder Bay to the rail line.

By paying attention to the various types of occupations available to Indian workers through the years, general trends become discernible in the development process. Casual or seasonal employment, for example, has become less prevalent as demand increases for more regular, full-time employment. In conjunction with this new preference, such activities as trapping, hunting, and fishing, while still important, require much less time and effort than in the pre-snowmobile and motor boat period. This is especially true for the more affluent Indian workers who have the resources to most effectively exploit aquatic and faunal cycles, and thereby reduce costs through country food production.

Other forms of casual employment which were quite prevalent until a few years ago, such as berry picking, fire fighting, and tree planting, now have little preference among Indian workers. In fact, Collins leaders have told government officials that they will no longer tolerate the conscription of young men in their community for fire fighting. The Collins argument was that the construction of the tourist lodge at Whitewater Lake was crucial to the community's long-term development goals, and that the attainment of these goals would be compromised by the indiscriminate commandeering of local workers. Presumably the Ministry of Natural Resources now recruits fire fighters from the more isolated, less economically developed regions of the North where there still exists a demand for wage employment of this kind.

In terms of types of economic activities and occupations, the northern Indian work force can be characterized by four identifiable categories (Figure 4). It should be noted though, that these categories are not discrete units with neatly prescribed boundaries, but are used here as a heuristic device to depict a sequence over time. From this perspective economic change can be viewed as a process whereby individuals and groups progress through a series of different activities and occupations.

(1) *Subsistence-related activities* are exemplified by trapping, hunting, fishing, berry picking, domestic handicraft production, and firewood collection. These types of activities were prevalent forms of work for northern Indians until about 1930 when population growth and diminishing fur resources led to some displacement from their hunting economy. In later years an improvement in medical facilities and the construction of schools contributed to more sedentary communities. This decreased mobility has tended to reduce the use of country resources and related activities. By the 1970s men over forty years of age were the main trappers, but mostly they engaged in this activity only in conjunction with other economic pursuits. In Collins 25 percent of the work force is engaged predominantly in these forms of casual employment, and earnings tend to fall under $3,000 per year.

FIGURE 4

Changing Involvement of Ojibwa Work Force in Various Categories of Employment

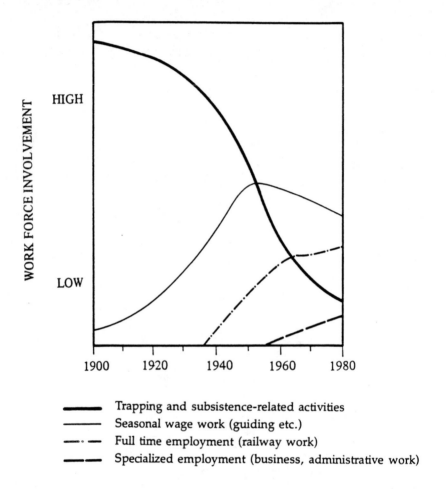

Trapping and subsistence-related activities
Seasonal wage work (guiding etc.)
Full time employment (railway work)
Specialized employment (business, administrative work)

(2) *Seasonal wage work* refers to activities such as guiding, fire fighting, tree planting, ice cutting, sawmill work, and construction. As outlined earlier some Indians worked as guides and freight transporters for fur traders during the last two centuries. But in this century there has been an ever-increasing number of outsiders entering the North for work and recreation who are in need of Indian services for the summer months. This form of employment has declined somewhat from a peak in the 1950s when many native people, with the decline of trapping during the winter, sought more permanent employment.

About 45 percent of the Collins work force is employed in seasonal employment of the type listed above, and annual incomes range from about $3,000 to $6,000 for such workers.

(3) *Permanent or regular full time employment* is usually work in such fields as caretaking and railway maintenance. For the most part Ojibwa of the Collins-Fort Hope area began to work for the CNR after leaving their trap lines in the early 1950s, a time when there was a strong demand for maintenance workers and railway crews in comparison to current requirements. But since the automation program of the 1960s, coupled with the arrival of the diesel engine, labour needs on the railway have been drastically reduced. Workers on full time jobs earn about $8,000 to $12,000 annually and constitute nearly 20 percent of the Collins work force.

(4) *Specialized full-time employment* includes various clerical and service occupations (secretarial, accounting, teaching, retail business, and community administration). Just under 10 percent of Collins workers are so employed, and they earn the highest annual incomes which range from $10,000 to $15,000. In Collins this group mainly comprises the McTavish family.

In sum, only about 30 percent of the Collins labour force (about 15 workers) is employed full time throughout the year and people in this category earn the highest wages. The remaining 70 percent (33 workers) do not have steady jobs, and workers in this case generally earn under $6,000 a year. From this discussion of types of economic activities engaged in by members of the Collins labour force, one might suggest that future improvements in the local economies of northern Indians will require the movement of workers away from the overcrowded, low income, resource-based occupations in which they now work into better paid, waged and salaried employment in other industries. In fact, this became somewhat of a standard recommendation (cf. Hawthorn 1966: 141), but what is usually overlooked are the special problems associated with the relocation of Indian workers and their families in northern areas.

Geographical Mobility

It is commonly thought that mobility, in the sense of a prolonged absence or permanent break from the home community, tends to reduce local population pressure on resources and existing job opportunities. In turn, a mobile labour force contributes to greater efficiency and higher per capita incomes because workers' mobility allows them to exploit outside labour markets, including more lucrative job openings. Of course, labour mobility only leads to these effects when there are significant differences in employment levels from one region to another. Few benefits are likely to accrue to workers who move to regions of relatively high unemployment.

The problem that is not often directly confronted is an important issue dealing with the relationship between labour mobility and community development. How can economic development, for example, be balanced with the social demands of village life? How can economic growth in small communities be stimulated without destroying a desire for increased local autonomy, or a determination to survive as distinct cultural groups? Will an emphasis on migration and relocation by authorities in the outside society drain small communities of their better educated and more productive members? Answers to these sorts of questions are critically important to any theory dealing with change in small populations. However, it should not be implied that Indian people are against mobility per se, for as hunters and trappers they have been an exceptionally mobile population. The reports of fur traders abound in references to the mobility of Ojibwa, Cree, and other northern hunters. Native people travelled vast distances along the major river systems to reach English posts on Hudson Bay, or French centres on Lake Superior. But even when trade was extended to many interior locations by the nineteenth century, Indian trappers would frequently by-pass nearby posts in favour of distant competitors who offered a better deal either in quantity or quality of trade goods. Local traders may have regarded such mobility as an indication of Indian disloyalty, but the latter were simply taking advantage of better economic opportunities as they saw them.

Migrants to the Collins area continued this tradition of mobility for the sake of better opportunities. During the first half of the twentieth century Ojibwa migrants from the North were motivated by two factors—one "push," and the other "pull." The "push" effect stemmed from mobility to escape the limited opportunities associated with declining faunal resources, a situation aggravated by a burgeoning reserve population. The "pull" effect was mobility in the search for better trading deals for some, and new forms of employment for others, such as railway construction, survey work, and mining jobs. Collins was a nexus for such activities, and provided the added advantage of low-cost store goods.

After 1950 geographical mobility was more restricted than in previous decades, and the Collins population coalesced about the trading post and CNR section houses. Resources in the immediate area of Collins were heavily taxed by the influx of migrants and, as a result, such activities as trapping, hunting, berry picking, and fishing became less productive. To complicate this situation the railway was steadily automating its maintenance program. In the days of coal burning locomotives (1910-1955), a foreman and four or five section men were stationed every seven miles or so. Today an equal number of men patrol twenty or more miles of track. Additionally, local labour is no longer required to operate the water tanks, coal docks, and rail switches. Unemployment and an uncertain resource base contributed to a stabilization in mobility for the Collins work force.

New opportunities over the next two decades (1955-1975) led to two new patterns of labour mobility. First, there was the short term variety of casual employment—guiding, fire fighting, tree planting—which drew workers away from the home community for only a few weeks or months. In general these jobs were low paying, and workers' families usually remained in the village. Second, there are jobs which are relatively permanent, which require relocation of the entire family, and for which remuneration is high. Railway work, involving the movement of men from one CNR section to another, is the predominant variety of this type of mobility. The usual motivation for workers to move away from the Collins section is to increase job security—to secure a job requiring a "bid," or to advance in the organization when positions are closed or do not exist in the worker's home area. One advantage of this type of work is the relative ease with which workers can return to Collins for short term visits, because of the reduced transportation costs for railroad employees.

Despite advantages of a regular paying job on the railway, many Collins workers have little desire to remain separated from kin, friends, and familiar surroundings for an indefinite period of time. In other words, there exists a conflict between the demands of village life and the demands of the labour market. Most Collins men have been employed on the railroad at one time or another, but when a man is requested to transfer to another section "down the line," he frequently tenders his resignation. Some men indicate that a transfer to a new section limits their enjoyment of off-hour activities, especially when they were not familiar with hunting grounds and fishing sites in their new surroundings. Other workers indicate that "the company owns you," referring to periods of enforced overtime—"you can't sleep when there's a train wreck," they said. One young man had progressed to the job of section foreman, but lost his job when he went to visit relatives at Cat Lake (about three hundred miles from Collins) during his holidays. To his misfortune winter arrived early and he was stranded at Cat Lake for the better part of a month. Although he had many years of steady, reliable service with the company, he was discharged from his position even before his return to Collins.

Another factor reducing occupational and geographic mobility in the Collins area is that the mobility of outside CNR employees (European immigrants and whites from southern Canada) has actually created new job opportunities for local workers. For the most part eastern Canadian and European immigrants comprised the majority of railway workers in northern Ontario, especially up to the 1950s. But these people did not regard "the bush" as home, and often sought a transfer out of the area at the first opportunity. Although this Eurocanadian population was living in isolation by their standards, the railway did provide rapid communication with the outside world, and they tended to have more knowledge than local people about outside job opportunities. For white immigrants advancement to such positions as section foreman, roadmaster or maintainer was an important step because not only did it mean a higher wage, it also meant a chance to transfer to a more populated area where outside goods and services were more readily available. As the number of immigrants who were willing to live and work in northern rural areas decreased, Indian workers began to fill the vacant positions, a process which corresponded with the sharp decline of fur trapping in the fifties.

In contrast to Eurocanadian railway employees, the highest supervisory position usually sought by native workers is that of section foreman. But in order to more fully understand workers' aspirations in both groups one must give some thought to the nature of local opportunity costs. Collins Ojibwa desire to work in proximity to kin and friends. They realize that a transfer to another section on the CNR could mean high rents, taxes, and new social problems—a higher cost of living with the probability of decreased buying power, which would offset possible wage gains. In Collins, workers usually own their own houses and are able to reduce subsistence costs by local hunting and fishing. Since Collins section men would probably lose these important advantages if they transferred out, workers often resign their railway jobs when CNR management pressures them to relocate in another district.

Income Distribution

During the course of field work a record was kept on annual incomes and their distribution for the entire Collins labour force. The ages of workers ranged from sixteen to eighty-seven years, and workers at these extremes had the lowest incomes (Table 6). The most significant wage earners in the village are men between the ages of twenty-one to forty. People in this age group made over 75 percent of cash earned through wage work, yet they comprise just over one-half of all workers. This group of young men actively seek wage labour for most of the year, and for the most part have young growing families. Conversely, men over forty years of age prefer to work on subsistence-related activities more than younger workers, and prefer to seek employment on a part-time basis when subsistence resources are at their lowest ebb. People under twenty years of age make up about 10 percent of the labour force, and prefer to continue their education where possible. In addition to the male workers, five women were employed in the kitchen and the store at Whitewater Lake and earned an average of about $700 each. This was the only instance of women earning wages.

TABLE 6

Wage Earner's Age, Sex, and Income, Collins 1974

Age group	Number Men	Women	Total wage income	Percent of total	Average income per worker
15-20	4	1	$14,005	8.9	$2,801
21-30	13	3	56,535	36.0	3,533
31-40	12	—	67,245	42.8	5,604
41-50	3	—	5,620	3.6	1,873
51-60	3	—	6,542	4.2	2,181
over 60	4	1	7,136	4.5	1,427
Totals	39	5	$157,083	100.0	$3,570

A more specific picture of the distribution of wage incomes in the Collins economy can be shown by using a "Lorenz curve," which shows cumulative relationships between levels of earned income and the percentage of workers in various income brackets (Figure 5). The resulting graph gives an indication of the extent of equality or inequality in the distribution of cash income in an economy. For the Collins economy wage incomes tend to be unevenly distributed as 80 percent of Collins workers received only 50 percent of the community's wage income total. In other words, only a small portion of the population (20%) controls a substantial sector of Collins spending power.

All sources of income for Collins people are shown in Table 7. Wages and other forms of earnings account for about three-quarters of the cash entering the community, while the remaining quarter is derived from transfer payments of various sorts, the most prominent of which are old age pensions and family allowance benefits. Sources of earned income can be divided into three categories:

(1) Income generated by Ogoki River Guides Ltd., the community development corporation which is the effective leadership body in Collins, amounted to about $85,000 (39 percent of the total income) for three projects. The main project was the construction of a tourist lodge at Whitewater Lake which employed a total of sixty-one men and

women, twenty-seven of whom were from Collins. Incomes derived
from this venture ranged to a high of $7,800 for a total of about $56,000.
The second largest project was the construction of a winter cargo road
to Whitewater Lake which employed twenty-two men who altogether
earned $22,300. A small project designed to explore possibilities for the
development of an Indian crafts industry employed fourteen people
whose total earnings amounted to $6,400.

FIGURE 5

**Lorenz Curve Showing Distribution of Wage Income among Collins
Workers, 1974**

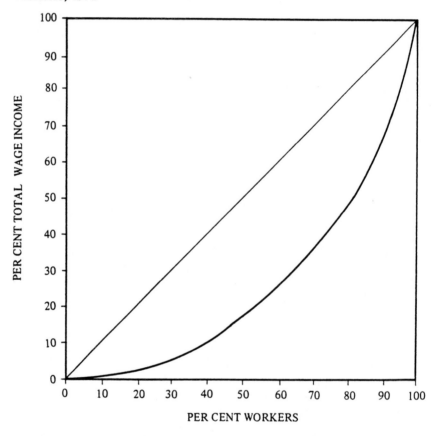

(2) Income derived from railway work amounted to nearly
$52,000 (24 percent of the total income). The CNR employs a core
section crew of five men who earn from $8,000 to $12,000 per year.

(3) Income earned while working at part-time activities such as
trapping, guiding, and the manufacture of handicrafts amounted to
about $29,000 (or 13 percent of the total income).

TABLE 7

Sources of Cash Income, Collins 1974

			Percent total
Earned income			
Government-sponsored projects			
(1) lodge construction	$56,232		
(2) winter roads	22,357		
(3) Indian crafts	6,394		
		84,983	39.0
CNR employment		52,100	23.9
Business		12,000	5.5
Guiding, ice-cutting		8,000	3.7
Adult education program		6,400	2.9
Fur trapping		1,600	0.7
Handicrafts		800	0.4
		165,883	76.1
Transfer payments			
Old age pension		18,360	8.4
Widow's allowance		15,000	6.9
Family allowance benefits		14,784	6.8
Unemployment insurance		2,000	0.9
Temporary relief/welfare		1,500	0.7
Treaty annuity		500	0.2
		52,144	23.9
		$218,027	100.0

Unearned income or transfer payments contributed about $52,000 (or 24 percent of the total income) to the Collins economy. Old age pensions were first extended to northern Indians around 1950, and at the time of this survey there were nine people over the age of sixty-five who were issued a monthly pension cheque for $140, many of whom also received an extra $30 as the "guaranteed income supplement." Family allowance benefits began in 1945, and provided about $22 a month for each child under the age of sixteen (or eighteen if the person was still attending school). In 1974 six widows in Collins received an allowance of $2,500 per annum, one family received temporary relief amounting to $1,000, and two persons benefited from unemployment insurance payments amounting to $2,000. In addition, all treaty Indians in Collins received $5 per year in annuity payments which began in 1905 when the Ojibwa signed Treaty 9 with the Canadian government.

In all, the average household receives about $4,800 in earnings and $1,500 in transfer payments per annum. Table 8 takes the distribution of cash income a step further by showing the distribution of both forms (earned and transfer) of cash income among Collins's thirty-four households. Slightly over half of the households have a gross annual income of less than $6,000, the range being from $1,000 to $22,000. An important factor contributing to this household income range is that some households have more than one wage earner: seven households have two workers and one has three workers. In general, household incomes rise with increases in the number of workers as one would expect, but the average income per worker in each category actually declines as the worker/household ratio increases. One reason for this situation is that multiple-worker households usually have some workers who have not reached, or are past, their peak earning power and who are primarily engaged in part-time work, such as summer employment for students, or trapping and guiding for older men.

TABLE 8

Distribution of Cash Income per Household, Collins 1974

Range ($)	Number	Percent
0-2,000	3	8.8
2,001-4,000	11	32.4
4,001-6,000	4	11.8
6,001-8,000	6	17.7
8,001-10,000	7	20.6
over 10,000	3	8.8

Consumption and Expenditure

Consumption can be defined as the utilization of material goods and services for the satisfaction of human needs and desires. In addition, it is important to distinguish between consumer goods and capital goods. A consumer good is one used by an individual for pleasure, that is, something that satisfies a human desire directly, while a capital good is used for the creation of additional wealth for its owner. Since the distinction is one of use, we can see that some goods, such as snowmobiles, can be used for both pleasure and business.

For any individual in Collins the gratification of human needs, such as food, clothing, or housing, takes place in the context of the household. People obtain and use the things they need because they are participants in particular households. In all, there is considerable variation in the patterns of household consumption in Collins, from the stark, one-room cabins of some elderly people, to the well-furnished dwellings of businessmen and political leaders. But despite these differences there are uniformities in the range of consumption and expenditure patterns, and it is towards these regularities that the present discussion is headed. One such regularity is that the organization of expenditure and consumption at the household level tends to be controlled by men, as household heads. As a general rule it is the household head who dispenses incoming cash and subsistence resources, although women are responsible for the proceeds of their own work, such as the production of handicrafts.

Clothing. In most areas of the world clothing is not a major expense, and does not form a significant portion of consumer demand. But in the arctic and subarctic regions of the world, warm clothing is an obvious necessity. The most preferred clothing is light, yet warm and durable. The new synthetic fabrics lined with down-fill are most desirable, such as parkas, mitts, sleeping bags, and even down-filled socks and underwear. These new articles of clothing, though, are mainly used in response to the new conditions created by snowmobile travel. The clothing problem is complicated by the high proportion of school-age children in the Collins population.

Housing. Permanent housing in Collins coincided with the construction of the Indian Affairs school in 1960. Prior to this time the population generally lived in canvas tents during the summer months at Collins Lake, then moved on to their trapping grounds in the interior for the winter. All residences in Collins, with the exception of the teacherage and CNR section houses, are of log construction. The houses are kept in good repair for the most part, and usually consist of one large room with a small wood stove in the centre for cooking and heating. A common practice is to move the stove outdoors during the summer, which serves to keep the cabin cool and the flies outside. In winter, heat is conserved by the use of a low roof and few windows. A small table with a few chairs is often propped up under a main window. Depending upon the size of the family, one or two beds line the walls. The beds, which are often covered with home-made quilts, or commercially produced sleeping bags or blankets, are commonly used as couches. Few families can afford fuel oil, and consequently most houses are wood heated. Coal oil lamps and candles are used for lighting. Cardboard is often nailed to the inside walls for added insulation.

In all, house construction is not a major expense for Collins people, but maintenance costs can be high especially for those using any form of fossil fuels for lighting or heating. One must also consider the hidden costs, such as the labour involved in hauling water and cutting firewood, when there is a lack of running water and electricity. Most houses do not last very long by southern standards; fifteen years seems to be the upper limit. The cost of repairs is high, considering the transportation costs of externally manufactured household materials, such as plywood, windows, and doors.

Transportation. In the Collins area transportation is by train, bush plane, boat, and snowmobile. The recent increases in oil and gasoline prices are an added expense for northern people. The passenger train is the usual mode of travel up and down the line, but there is only one arrival each day which means that one must find accommodations when visiting another town or village. Travel by aircraft is relied on by local people to reach interior fishing, trapping, and hunting sites, and the rates are expensive. The charge for a Cessna ride is 65 cents per mile, while the Turbo Otter carries a rate of $1.35 per mile load.

Equipment. The purchase of equipment is one area where the expression of consumer demand is most pronounced. All households have equipment which is considered a necessity for subsistence activities, such as fish net, knives, axes, guns, tents, and a canoe. In addition, there are other items which are considered close to indispensable, such as an outboard motor, power saw, shot gun, sleeping bags, angling gear, and a snowmachine. A short list of new items of Eurocanadian technology would include nineteen snowmachines, nine propane and naptha stoves, four gas generators, four oil stoves, and three television sets (although reception from Thunder Bay is virtually non-existent).

Store Food. My discussions with the people of Collins indicate that it has only been since the 1940s that there has been any reliance at all on outside foods. Over this thirty-year period such items as sugar, flour, potatoes, salt, and tea remain staples in the store-bought diet of northern Ojibwa along with country foods (Table 9). Yet by the 1970s, fresh meat, fruit, and vegetables have become a prominent aspect of consumer demand, partly because of accessibility (because Collins is on the rail line), but also because consumers can now afford to purchase such produce. The prominent pattern, however, is for residents to rely on the local store for food heavy in carbohydrates but low in protein (about 40,000 lbs. of sugar, flour, and potatoes are imported annually). In all, Collins people spend about $60,000 on food annually, some of which is spent at other stores along the rail line (mainly Armstrong, Savant Lake, and Sioux Lookout) where there is a greater variety of consumer goods than can be found at the Collins store. Even trappers transport much of their food from the local store to the trap line, but since the time spent in the bush has decreased steadily in recent years there has been a corresponding increase in the dependence on store food.

TABLE 9

Average Monthly Sales by Collins Store, 1974

Item	Quantity	Wholesale value	% total
Sugar	1,500 lbs.	$647	
Flour	1,000	141	
Potatoes	700	110	
Lard	540	251	
Pork chops	420	474	
Eggs	375	270	
Apples	320	65	
Oranges	320	53	
Onions	301	30	
Bacon	273	213	
Chicken	247	183	
Bologna	240	152	
Bread	230	98	
Ham	180	190	
Beef steakettes	168	155	
Veal steakettes	150	147	
Macaroni	144	52	
Baking powder	120	80	
Butter	100	86	
Sirloin steak	84	170	
Candy and biscuits	50	40	
Weiners	48	33	
Tomatoes	40	16	
Salt	10	15	
Tea	6	113	
	7,566 lbs. (3,439 kgs.)	$3,784	65.9
Canned milk	1,200 tins	332	
Pork and beans	480	233	
Beef stew	360	205	
Peaches	360	145	
Canned meat	240	120	

TABLE 9—continued

Item	Quantity	Wholesale value	% total
Spaghetti	240	78	
Corn	240	76	
Chicken stew	120	68	
	3,240 tins		1,257	21.9
Powdered drinks		220	
Toilet tissue		94	
Laundry soap		73	
Syrup		31	
Dish soap		20	
Hand soap		18	
Laundry bleach		15	
Batteries		15	
			486	8.5
Cigarettes (40 cartons)		152	
Snuff (10×8 rolls)		34	
Tobacco (10×1.5 oz)		29	215	3.7
			$5,742	100.0

Source: This table is based on order forms for replacement stocks kindly made available to me by the Collins store owner for April to September, 1974.

In order to provide the reader with a more specific picture of consumption patterns for food I used order forms for stock replacement from the Collins store as an indicator of monthly food sales. This monthly sales table was then broken down into such categories as carbohydrates, meat, fruit and vegetables, and dairy products, in terms of the average household consumption per month (Table 10). As the table shows, for the average household about an equal amount is spent on each of carbohydrates, meat, and fruit/vegetables/dairy products, but the cash saved by eating country meat tends to exceed that spent on store meat. By volume, the average household consumes about 120 lbs. of carbohydrates, 110 lbs. of meat, 80 lbs. of fruit and vegetables, and 50 lbs. of dairy products per month. Thus, in terms of most nutritional standards Collins people have a fairly high protein diet per month. But should the trend towards increased reliance on store food continue, and if incomes do not rise substantially in the future, one can expect a higher carbohydrate, and less nutritious, diet to predominate with decreased utilization of country foods.

TABLE 10

Household Food Consumption per Month, Collins 1974-75

Item	Total Population/Mo.		Household/Mo.[a]	
	Volume/lbs.	Value/$	Volume/lbs.	Value/$
Carbohydrates	4,184	1,540	123	45
Meat (a) store	2,050	1,837	60	54
(b) bush[b]	1,622	3,633	48	107
Fruits and vegetables	2,761	768	81	23
Dairy Products	1,675	688	49	20
Totals	12,292	$8,466	361	$249
	(5,531 kg)		(163 kg)	

[a] Calculations are for thirty-four households.
[b] Bush meat includes fish and fowl, see Table 13.

Household Budgets

An examination of household budgets further illustrates the consumption patterns of Collins people. The first example (Table 11) is that of a Nipigon House family of five children and two adults. One-half of this family's income is derived from casual wage work (mainly guiding) and the other half from transfer payments. The total income averages $763 per annum per consumer. Most of this family's income is allotted for food and clothing (about 80 per cent of the budget), which leaves little for expenditures on capital equipment, thus affecting this family's ability to secure subsistence resources, although fish are relied upon during the guiding season.

The second household is a Fort Hope family (Table 12) whose income is derived principally from a steady job on the CNR, supplemented with construction work (during the worker's vacation period) and trapping. By contrast, the average income per consumer in this family ($1,610) is over twice that of the previous family and is thus close to the community-wide average (the per capita income was $1,678 for 1974). Also, by contrast with the former household discussed, food and clothing expenditures for this second household amount to about 60 percent of the family's budget. Expenditure on equipment and household supplies amounts to almost 40 percent for the Fort Hope family's budget, while only 13 percent for the Nipigon House household. Thus, the accumulation of household equipment is considerably larger for the Fort Hope family and is reflected somewhat in their higher trapping income. Also, the Fort Hope family has a possibility to save about 8 percent of its income, while the Nipigon group labours slightly in debt (at about 4 percent).

TABLE 11

Estimated Household Budget, Nipigon House Family of Seven Persons, 1974

1. *Income*			
Wages	$3,007		
Family Allowance	1,200		
Temp. relief	1,000		
Trapping	100		
Treaty annuity	35		
	$5,342		
Taxes	—		
Disposable income	5,342		$5,342
2. *Expenditures*		%	
a. Food	3,300	59	
b. Clothing	1,200	22	
c. Household			
Gasoline	240		
Furnishing	70		
Maint./repairs	50		
	360	6	
d. Miscellaneous			
Equipment	200		
Entertainment	100		
Travel	50		
Sundries	50		
	400	7	
e. Capital depreciation	329	6	
		100%	$5,589
			debt: $247
			(4% debt)

Depreciation on Household Equipment

Item	Value	Life-span (years)	Annual depreciation
Snowmachine	$1,200	5	$240
Stove	50	5	10
Gas generator	150	10	15
Power saw	200	10	20
Axes	30	5	6
Fish net	30	5	6
Tent	70	5	14
Rifle	270	15	18
	$2,000		$329

TABLE 12

Estimated Household Budget, Fort Hope Family of Eight Persons, 1974

1. *Income*				
Wages	$11,206			
Family allowance	1,140			
Trapping	500			
Treaty annuity	40			
		$12,886		
Taxes, federal	1,445			
provincial	486	1,931		
Disposable income		10,955		$10,955
2. *Expenditures*			%	
a. Food		4,200	42	
b. Clothing		1,600	16	
c. Household				
Fuel Oil	1,500			
Gasoline	400			
Propane	150			
Furnishings	130			
Maintenance	100			
Repairs	—			
		2,280	23	
d. Miscellaneous				
Equipment	500			
Entertainment	500			
Travel	300			
Sundries	200			
		1,500	15	
e. Capital depreciation		549	5	
			101%	10,129

Possible savings: $826

Depreciation on Household Equipment

Item	Value	Life-span (years)	Annual depreciation
Snowmachine	$1,200	5	$240
Boat	700	10	70
Motor (7.5 hp)	400	10	40
Television	300	5	60
Rifle (30/30)	270	15	18

TABLE 12—continued

Item	Value	Life-span (years)	Annual depreciation
Rifle (.22)	100	15	6
Shotgun (12 g.)	175	15	12
Power saw	200	10	20
Gas generator	150	10	15
Stoves (cook)	100	10	10
(heat)	50	5	10
Tent	70	5	14
Sleeping bags	50	5	10
Radio	40	5	8
Fishing rods, etc.	40	10	4
Fish net	30	5	6
Axes	30	5	6
	$3,905		$549

Subsistence Resources

Over the last three centuries northern Indians have undergone a slow process of integration into, and dependence upon, the outside world. But for the most part northern Indians have remained on the margin of the Eurocanadian social and economic system—what Dunning (1959a) has called "acculturation at a distance." Today, contacts with the outside are accelerating, especially in the areas of education, wage employment, and government subsidy. Yet complete incorporation into the wider society seems unlikely in view of the isolation of many communities and some basic conflicts between wage work and the demands of village life. One conflict stems from the fact that full-time jobs are mostly absent in the small communities, and so long periods away from home mean a difficult family life. Another conflict is between country food production, a necessary activity to support life in many northern native settlements, and the need for money to purchase other essentials. The trade-offs are not easily resolved, especially when both cash and bush food are scarce resources.

My interest in this problem stems from a conversation I had about a decade ago with an elderly Ojibwa woman. We were talking about an old friend of hers who had refused further treatment at the Sioux Lookout Hospital because the doctors had prohibited her from eating pickerel, a staple in her friend's diet for most of her life. We talked further about hunting and fishing, and then she closed the conversation with, "You know, cows were made for white people—moose for Indians. An Indian eats cows and pigs, and dies." It struck me that hunting is more than an activity of symbolic importance.

If one were to place a monetary value on bush food, then subsistence production in Collins would contribute over $40,000 to the local economy (Table 13). Moose are by far the most important source of meat and account for about one-half of all country food production, while fish and waterfowl make up another third of the total. There is no animal that rivals the moose in the estimation of northern Ojibwa. Old people claim that one's health will deteriorate without an adequate supply of moose meat. Each grown animal provides over three hundred pounds of edible meat, and therefore the return on productive effort is relatively high. Most moose are killed in the fall and winter, usually by high powered rifles. Occasionally people relate that moose are killed in the summer when they are found swimming across a lake and are thus easy prey. Besides meat, moose also provide an important source of hides for coats, mitts, and moccasins.

TABLE 13

Estimated Country Food Production, Collins 1974-75

Species	Total catch	lbs. edible[a] food each	Total lbs. edible food	Value[b] ($)
Moose	25	330.2	8,255	20,637
Beaver	100	12.7	1,270	3,175
Bear	3	189.0	567	1,418
Rabbit	300	1.6	480	1,200
Caribou	2	104.9	210	525
Martin	25	5.0	125	312
Otter	5	8.4	42	105
Muskrat	15	1.1	16	40
Mink	5	0.8	4	10
Waterfowl	1,500	2.5	3,750	6,750
Partridge	500	0.7	350	630
Pickerel	3,000	1.0	3,000	6,000
Lake Trout	300	4.0	1,200	2,400
Sturgeon	50	3.9	195	390
Totals			19,464 lbs. (8,847 kgs.)	$43,592

[a] The edible food equivalents are from Elberg *et al*. (1975).
[b] The cash values are derived from Usher's (1976: 104) substitution figures of $2.50/lb. fresh meat, $1.80/lb. for birds, and $2.00/lb. for fish.

Beaver are one of the most economically important animals as they yield the highest pelt value and second highest source of edible meat which, like the moose, is highly esteemed. Beaver are usually taken in steel traps during the winter and spring, although they are sometimes shot with small calibre rifles.

Next to the moose, bears provide the highest proportion of edible meat per animal, but bear meat is not greatly desired. Although they are fairly numerous in the area, bears are not usually hunted but are shot when they become a nuisance to the village. Of the other large animals caribou are occasionally shot but, since their virtual disappearance from the area some thirty or forty years ago, they are rarely seen today. Rabbits are one of the most important small animals sought by Collins people. They are usually snared by women and teenagers in the winter close to the village, and at least three hundred are caught annually. In former times the numbers caught appeared to be in the thousands, especially since rabbit skins were used for blankets, coats, and mitt liners.

Game birds are a significant source of protein in the diet and yield about four thousand pounds of meat annually. Ducks and geese are mainly shot in the fall and spring during their migration periods. Some families set up special camps at a favourite site in early May when these birds, restricted to small areas of open water, are easily dispatched with shot guns. Partridge or grouse, of which about five hundred are killed a year, are hunted during the fall when large numbers are sometimes found in a small area. During the summer months fish are basic to the diet of Collins people, the most important of which are pickerel, lake trout, and sturgeon. Gill nets are usually used for fishing, although angling has become somewhat of a novelty among the more affluent members of the community.

The gathering of wild plants and berries provides only seasonal variety to the diet of Collins people. During August women and children can be found collecting large quantities of blueberries, but these are usually for immediate consumption. In former times blueberries were an important source of cash income for a family, but now there are fewer forest fires which tend to rejuvenate berry patches. Also, since berry picking is labour intensive and prices per basket have not risen substantially since the 1950s, there is little incentive to invest one's labour in picking when more lucrative casual work can be found in the summer. Labrador Tea is sometimes collected, but mainly by older people for medicinal purposes.

Now that the sources and volume of bush food in the Collins economy has been outlined, we are now in a position to ascertain the impact that variations in cash income and country food production have on each other. To this end data from other Indian communities was tabulated on per capita income levels, and on the quantity of meat consumed per day. For the purposes of this comparison the Ojibwa village of Collins was compared with three Cree communities on the James Bay coast, namely Fort George, Paint Hills, and Eastmain (Table 14). The results surprised me.

TABLE 14

Income and Fresh Meat Consumption

Community	lbs. meat/ person/day	Per capita income
Fort George	1.38	$1,190
Collins	1.20[a]	1,680[b]
Paint Hills	0.28	990
Eastmain	0.64	890

[a] Meat consumption for Collins people was calculated using figures of 1.0 for individuals over 16 years, and 0.5 for those under 16 years. Slightly different computations were used by Elberg *et al.* (1975) for the Cree communities, but this difference should have a negligible effect on the overall results.

[b] Collins per capita income would have been $1,025 without the government-sponsored projects in 1974.

My initial assumption was that rising incomes in a community, which is the case with the four villages in the chart, would lead to decreased utilization of country food. The reasoning was that if people could afford to buy more store bought food, they would do just that. Only those with low incomes, the argument might go, would continue to hunt and fish. But the reasoning was all wrong; the table shows that a different relationship exists—the higher the per capita cash income in these communities, the greater the amount of country meat consumed.

After rethinking events that occurred in Collins, it became evident that some of the most prolific hunters in the settlement were also those with the highest paying jobs. The reasoning now would be that rising incomes increase efficiency in country food production to the extent that those with high incomes can afford better hunting equipment and more frequent expeditions to remote, and less utilized, areas. A high income also allows the part-time hunter to make more effective use of peak periods in game cycles, such as fish spawns or geese migrations. These sources of country food are widely dispersed throughout most of the year and, aside from times when large numbers can be found, the return on productive effort is low. The most effective strategy then is to hunt and fish intensively during high points in faunal cycles, and work for cash when the highest paying jobs are available. Unfortunately for northern Indian communities, the best times for hunting and working often overlap, as illustrated in Figure 6. Guiding, fire fighting, tree planting, construction work, and railway maintenance are all occupations that absorb the most workers during peak hunting and fishing times.

FIGURE 6

Workers Employed Per Month, 1974

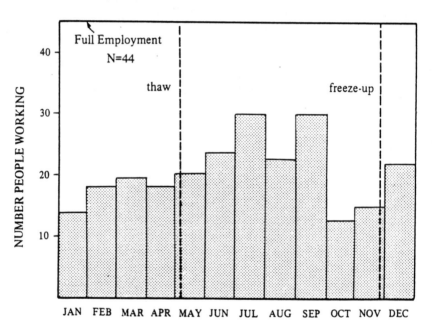

Those who have difficulty securing wage employment are doomed to a double dilemma—they have to hunt and fish when a return on their effort is uncertain, and yet they do not have the cash for expenditures on capital equipment, maintenance, and transportation costs to increase subsistence production. A research team from McGill University (the Anthropology of Development Program) has spent the last decade studying the impact of economic change on northern Cree, and their work on the Cree use of subsistence resources brings into sharper focus this dual-faceted dilemma:

Increasing expenditures on food would reduce the amount needed for capital investment and maintenance, and it is these expenses which involve the immense northern mark-up. Yet increased wage employment would not increase the cash income to the same effect. Once subsistence hunting is let go, the northern people are involved in a downward spiral of dependency, with wages in the north never catching up with the in-built inflation of prices in the area. Only to the extent that local resources can continue to be used by northern peoples do they have a buffer against this inflation, and an economic means of keeping northern prices down, and of ensuring that their labour is paid at a living wage (Elberg *et al*. 1975: 72).

It is obvious that northern Indians run a perilous treadmill in their attempts to guard against the replacement of a high quality country meat diet by a diet of low quality store-bought carbohydrates, without seriously lowering health and nutrition standards.

One conclusion stemming from this discussion is that part-time activity in both the subsistence resource and wage work sectors of northern Indian economies helps maintain basic nutritional standards. Such a strategy also allows for investment in capital equipment, the possibilities of which would decrease significantly if northern people were to rely solely on expensive store-bought foods. It is for this reason that small increases in wage employment in the North may actually reduce workers' annual incomes because such increases may fall below the cash value of subsistence hunting and fishing. The structure of opportunity costs in the North further suggests that any plans to initiate economic change in Indian communities, such as increasing employment, will be less than successful unless:

(1) a substitute can be found for the protein-rich country food, one which would not cause expenditures above present hunting costs, and

(2) store foods, of sufficient quality to maintain a sound nutritional diet, were subsidized, at least to the point where there existed some parity between north-south food prices.

In sum, while any increase in earned income is a welcome sign in the North, the concept of "income" is meaningless unless one is referring to increases in *real income*. In most northern Indian communities income means wages *minus* lost subsistence production. To increase wages, but reduce the consumption of country food, leads to negligible rises in real income. As such, consideration of both sides of the equation (i.e., Income = Wages + Subsistence Production) is necessary to cause a true rise in the standard of living of northern peoples.

Conclusion

Over the last three centuries northern Indians have undergone three different phases of changing exchange relationships. In the first phase trading took place in the context of reciprocal gift-giving ceremonies. The important social unit during this period was the hunting group whose leader represented all members of the group in negotiations with European traders. The second phase was characterized by a direct exchange of furs for trade goods, first through "trading chiefs," then on an individual trapper basis. By the twentieth century there was a more complete transformation to non-reciprocal exchange. European entrepreneurs attempted to change Indian work concepts and labour arrangements to the European model characterized by a hierarchical ordering of role relationships. Europeans became the *okima* or bosses, negotiations took place directly between individual members of the Indian group and the trader, and there was a decline in the basis of support for native leaders. In all there was a shift from "exchanging labour" to "hiring labour" directly, and from reciprocal to non-reciprocal labour relationships. By the 1970s we find a more complete monetization of work, and concrete hourly rates with less emphasis on piece work in the local economy. Coupled with these changes has been a trend towards increased occupational diversification and full-time specialized employment.

The section on income and its distribution further demonstrates the increasing individualization of workers and households. The unequal distribution of cash income in the Collins community suggests a trend towards increased social and economic differentiation in the Indian population. In turn, as transfer payments amount to one-quarter of the total cash income for the community, this section also shows an increasing dependence on the governmental and economic institutions of the larger society. But this high level of subsidy, by contrast, also allows for a greater independence of those persons who would otherwise have to rely on the financial support of kinsfolk and friends, such as the elderly, the unemployed, widows, and the destitute. In a sense, they have become an added asset, rather than a burden, to the household. A related factor fostering socio-economic differentiation is that as household incomes have increased, so have opportunities for the purchase of new technology which allows for more efficient utilization of country resources by individual households. The cumulative effect of this trend in resources use is to undermine co-operative efforts outside of the household as extra labour and tools are less frequently in demand. Also, a continued reliance on store-bought food increases dependence on the outside economic system, and away from a need for the support of other households within the community. The positive effect is that higher cash incomes allow for the purchase of better subsistence equipment, and the opportunity to increase *real* incomes by reducing food costs.

CHAPTER FOUR

Emergent Leadership and Economic Opportunity

Canada has such a relatively small population in comparison to its land mass that communication of needs and desires by people from one part of the country to another has often constituted a problem. But problems of communication are not entirely a function of geographical distance. In order to process people's interests, and implement programs of action, access to the appropriate regulatory agency is required. In Canada, reserve Indians have available a structure of communication channels which allows them to deal directly with such a regulatory body—the Indian Affairs Branch. An Indian reserve has an elective body consisting of a chief and councillors through which the reserve Indian population can communicate its interests to higher levels of government.

A fundamental problem with this situation, as indicated in the "Hawthorn Report" (1966: 360-67), is that the Indian Affairs Branch has seen its role historically as protectors from abuse, rather than as innovators of economic and social change in Indian communities. Throughout most of its history the Indian Affairs Branch has adhered to an individual enfranchisement policy, and reserves tended to be viewed as training grounds in the Indian-to-white integration process (Ponting and Gibbins 1980: 16-30). "Graduation" from a reserve meant citizenship, and supposedly a ready access to all the rights and privileges to which citizens are entitled. The problem was that enfranchised Indians soon found that they lacked access to formal communication channels analogous to the Indian Affairs structure.

Actually this problem of access to government agencies and services is really part of a much broader issue dealing with the problem of local government for Indian communities. The "Hawthorn Report" did make a start in elucidating this matter by summarizing the main

79

problems of local Indian government as they were perceived in the mid-1960s. But the scope of this report was limited because, like the federal government, researchers working on the task force studied Indian problems only in terms of persons holding legal status. Thus, the problem of local government for Indians became the problem of developing government within the framework of the Indian Act. The writers of this report did not have a mandate to deal with non-status Indians and Métis. But as the Collins case exemplifies, these people were also struggling with the problems of local government, although for them problems were set in the context of municipal frameworks as established by provincial statutes.

To complicate matters for native people in non-reserve communities, government officials at the provincial level have been hesitant about implementing new programs, especially when there is the possibility of conflict over federal jurisdiction. At the community level there have not emerged, until recently, competent individuals willing to assume the responsibility for community development and for the task of pressing provincial agencies for community services. In part, as a consequence of this lack of identifiable community leadership and of the lack the accessible communication channels with higher levels of government, non-status and Métis people have generally not benefited from the basic services which most Canadians have come to take for granted. This chapter will show how the situation is changing in one particular non-reserve community, especially through channels of emergent leadership. It will try to isolate the strategies such leaders use to gain local support and to obtain benefits for followers.

The Emergence of Community Leadership

By the 1960s problems in the economic life of Collins people were reaching alarming proportions. Many families continued to struggle with the annual subsistence cycle of winter trapping and summer fishing, supplemented with periods of goose hunting and berry picking. Since the construction of the primary school in 1960, there was increased pressure on families for regular school attendance. Sometimes grandparents would remain in the village in order to look after the children, but most often children would remain in the bush with the household group for extended periods during the winter months. As a result of this situation of conflicting demands, trappers' fur production tended to decline because of the decreased amount of time spent in the bush, and the education of children suffered because of frequent absences from the settlement.

Social and economic instability went hand-in-hand. Economic instability stemmed from the peculiarities of the fur trade, the conditions of which varied with fluctuations in the supply of fur-bearers and unstable market prices. Figures available from the Ministry of Natural Resources, for example, show that the average price paid for beaver pelts during the 1945-46 season was $50.78, but within a decade the price had dropped to just $9.65 per pelt. This problem of declining fur prices since the 1950s is further exacerbated by the coincident rise in the cost of living in the North during the same period. For many it was evident that trapping no longer offered hope for economic security and material well-being, yet there existed few alternatives to trapping in the surrounding area. The situation bred frustration, anxiety, and a general uncertainty of existence.

For the most part, those who were dissatisfied with the dwindling monetary returns from trapping attempted to conform to a more settled life style by engaging in wage work and commercial fishing. But fishing required a considerable capital investment, which was usually lacking, and was restricted to lakes close to the railway because of transportation problems. For Collins people commercial fishing lasted for only a few years in the 1950s, partially due to a decline in the fish population, but also because of the lack of the development of an efficient marketing system to organize fishermen, to collect and store the catch, and to negotiate sales with southern wholesalers. Because Indians did not have the facilities to get the fish to market profitably, commercial licences drifted into the hands of white entrepreneurs. Also, workers with employment on the railroad found that new opportunities were restricted as the CNR began a program of automation. The change-over to diesel engines meant less maintenance work than when the old "smokers" ran the rails. Gone were the days of coal docks, water tanks, manual switches, and a large railway work force.

Leadership posed a further problem. Skills which made a trap line leader effective were less relevant in attempts to cope with the uncertainties of the outside world. The only overall patron in the community, a Scottish fur trader, had died during the mid-1960s, a time when his role in the trapping economy was diminishing. He had been in the fur business for most of his life, yet in his later years he had made an attempt to market local fish and blueberry production, and was instrumental in the construction of the primary school in Collins.

The decline of the fur business was a vexing problem for the trader-patron. His trading post had become established as a focus for social gatherings and residence of Collins-area Indians. Churches and the school strengthened ties to this focal point and, as Indians were drawn away from life in the bush to life in the community, there was a concurrent draining of support for native leaders. The trader had taken over the native-leader role as distributor of goods to followers, since this was no longer possible for native leaders on the trap lines as their resource base (furs and meat) was diminishing. In addition, native leaders suffered a loss in their religious and supernatural bases for support because of the rising influence of missionaries. The trader-patron had become an *okima*—a recognized leader among Indians—and had the authority of a chief. The problem was that a decline in native leadership was also coincident with a decline in the authority of traders, since both depended upon the fur trapping business as a basis for their authority and support. When trapping declined Indians moved to the settlement, but without a viable source of livelihood they would be unable to pay their bills at the store. Thus, it was in the trader-patron's best interest, indeed as a veritable tactic of survival, to find alternative sources of income for the population resident at Collins. This was a problem that he was unable to solve in his lifetime, and with which his sons are still grappling. However, before the trader's death he had embarked on a course of intensifying external contacts, while at the same time attempting to prevent defections from the local community.

The trader's crucial role during the 1950s and early 1960s, then, was to prevent the fragmentation of the Collins population during the difficult years between fur trapping and steady wage work. In order to accomplish this end most effectively, the trader was forced to diversify relationships with followers. In effect he was forced to change his single-stranded relations with trapper-followers to multi-stranded relations involving a wide diversity of services. Unless he controlled other sources of employment besides the fur trade, his influence would surely diminish. To this end the trader-patron hired men to cut firewood, to put up ice for the cold storage house, and to serve as guides for the increasingly large number of American hunters and fishermen who were beginning to penetrate the north country in the 1950s. He hired men to construct small tourist camps in the area, and women to work in the store. The trader organized work crews for fire fighting, survey work, and for work at the lumber mill at Fee's Spur, occasionally even lending equipment for such operations. His new pool room became a sort of "men's house" where people gathered to discuss current events in the community. The trader opened a post office, not only as a new source of income, but because it provided a focus for outside communication, along with the new pay phone that he had installed in the store. The post office became so popular in fact that postal money orders began to replace cash as a basis for transactions. A money order is just as negotiable as cash and, unlike money, is guaranteed against loss. In effect, the post office became a para-banking institution in Collins.

The trader was further active in establishing his burgeoning business complex as a focal point for itinerant Eurocanadians. Small rooms were partitioned beside the post office as a hostel where such "guests" as forestry officials, clergymen, Indian Affairs agents, or police officers were lodged. They usually stayed only a night or two, and were invariably fed at the trader's table. Conversations on various topics relating to the North were a frequent post-supper activity, but any mention of remuneration for these courtesies would be considered an insult. All that was required was that the guest keep the best interest of Collins people in mind. In most cases though, both parties benefited from the association. The problems of Collins were more widely advertised, and visitors gained from the knowledge of northern conditions imparted by the trader, an example being the case of politicians who sought grass-roots support and hoped that the trader's extensive contacts, knowledge, and influence would serve to fortify their campaigns.

As the importance of external associations increased, local people in turn became more dependent upon the trader's intercalary role. Higher incomes meant higher taxes, and many people sought his advice at income tax time. He kept a store of medical supplies and insisted that the health nurse make regular visits to the community. The trader also became responsible for issuing the welfare vouchers for needy families made available by the Department of Social and Family Services. Vouchers were usually exchanged for food and clothing at the store, and under these circumstances indebtedness relations continued in much the same manner as during the fur trade era. At election time the trader was the local enumerator and returning officer.

From the foregoing account it can be seen that the trader had come to influence, or ultimately control, access to the Indian community at Collins by various segments of Eurocanadian society—health and welfare, education, law enforcement, religion, politics, government administration, and commerce. The trader was an individual of relative wealth, generosity, and favourable connections, and no one thought to usurp his authority in local affairs. He was able to forge continual and multi-stranded indebtedness relations both inside and outside the community. As a transactional strategist the trader-patron was most effective, and he remained ensconced as a patron because, so to speak, he had clients on both sides of the fence. But even at the time of his death economic activity in the settlement had become fragmented and unco-ordinated, welfare dependency was on the rise, and unemployment had permeated the work force.

The Formation of Ogoki River Guides Ltd.

That the Collins community was in a crisis situation during the 1960s was most evident to the young people—those that had some schooling and familiarity with the outside world, coupled with a knowledge of the limitations of a trapping economy as a basis for coping with future problems. The death of the trader-patron left a leadership vacuum within the community, especially since his leadership was essentially an exercise in personal influence. Collins was now an acephalous community, at least until the return of the trader's three sons.

Possibly with a view to the future, the father had willed various portions of his property to each of his three sons, and for this reason there was some incentive for the sons to return to the Collins area. The eldest, Tom McTavish (pseudonyms are used for personal names), was in his late twenties at his father's death, and had just returned from a stint in the armed forces. The second son, John McTavish, was finishing a course in business college, and was given the store business. Allen McTavish, the third son, arrived home with training as a book-keeper from the CNR offices in Toronto. It was their conclusion that some variety of community council was a necessary first step towards extricating the Collins community from its current economic dilemma. Their first venture into the political arena began in 1968 with the formation of the "Collins Committee for Community Development." The Committee was launched in response to two immediate issues of the time—the installation of an electrical generator in the community, and the use of the school building for recreational purposes. But with the achievement of these rather limited goals, interest in the Committee began to dissipate. People wanted jobs first; entertainment later. Although the Committee was a forerunner of the more sophisticated Ogoki River Guides Ltd. which followed in the 1970s, it did provide a basis for the formulation of strategy and decision making which has continued to the present day—the mobilization of local labour, coupled with outside investment capital and expertise.

The most important aspect of the Committee overall was that it allowed for some training and exposure for the brothers in dealing with outside bureaucracies. With this experience behind them, the brothers set out to form a more perdurable organization for community action. In this regard the contacts forged years earlier by their father proved invaluable. They called in their father's political credits, so to speak, and held consultation meetings with lawyers, merchants, bankers, politicians, government agents, and clergymen. The consensus which emerged from these meetings was that a community development corporation should be formed—one that held a legal charter, one that was "non-profit" oriented, and one that allowed for membership and participation by all people in Collins. This advice was sound in a number of regards, especially since government agencies, from which funding would later be sought, would only deal with an appropriately chartered corporation, and one which represented the population of Collins as a whole. Lawyers drafted the charter for a nominal fee, some influential friends of the trader agreed to sit on the board of directors (which greatly enhanced ORG's credibility), and newspaper reporters wrote articles proclaiming the start of a new era for the Collins community.

By 1972 ORG was a bona fide corporation, and like other corporations it exhibits a multiplicity of leadership roles, the main ones being a president, secretary-treasurer, vice-president, and two other (outside) members of the board of directors. A most salient feature of this organization is that economic, political, and administrative roles are found within the same structural framework. In all, the division of authority in ORG is based on the following roles:

(1) The president (Tom McTavish) is responsible for maintaining contacts with outside officials, for negotiating the basis for external support in local projects, and for articulating the needs of everyone in the organization from worker to board member.

(2) The secretary-treasurer (John McTavish) has the task of ensuring the viability of community projects by maintaining the flow of outside resources, and by channeling these resources into the appropriate capital and labour expenditures.

(3) The bookkeeper (Allen McTavish) directs the cash flow to workers and, in turn, directs funds to various outside sources such as taxes, pension funds, medical insurance, and so on.

(4) The organizational structure is completed by three men who regularly act as foremen on ORG projects, and it is their responsibility to direct the activities of work crews on the job site.

In addition, it is worth noting that all local members of the board are also members of the majority Fort Hope group. The positions of president, secretary-treasurer, and bookkeeper are occupied by the three brothers, while the position of vice-president is held by an influential male affine to one of the brothers (i.e., the secretary-treasurer, John McTavish). The vice-president has considerable prestige in the community because he is also the local CNR section foreman, and is thus in a position to influence the few full-time wage earners in Collins who live independent of decisions made by the ORG executive. And probably most important of all, his position as vice-president ensures that the balance of power in ORG decision making remains in Collins. The two remaining members of the board of directors, a banker and clothing merchant in the distant community of Sioux Lookout, tend to function only in an advisory capacity.

In sum, over the last two decades there has been an increasing centralization of political and economic power in Collins. The trader-patron started a transition from fur trapping to wage labour. A more complex leadership structure emerged with the formation of ORG, which continued the transition by offering expanded wage work opportunities. Accordingly, each change in leadership was accompanied by an important innovation in the local economy. Economic success is therefore seen as an important factor in maintaining the power and authority of Collins leaders. In turn, a centralized authority structure promotes success by the efficient organization of work. Collins was fortunate in having leaders who were capable of planning the economy and organizing the labour force.

Collins Leaders

If you were to ask anyone who the most important person in Collins is, the answer in just about every case would be, "Tom McTavish." Tom is a heavy-set, forceful man who has been the main actor in making ORG a reality. People sometimes dislike him for his brashness, but when it comes to conflicts with government people Tom's uncanny ability to overwhelm the opposition makes him an ideal person for front-line duty. A forceful personality is one reason for Tom McTavish's success as a leader, but a more important source of his local status and authority are Tom's family connections. Tom's father, the Scottish fur trader, was a highly regarded man in northern Ontario, probably because he showed an independence of spirit (by quitting the HBC), married into an important Fort Hope Indian family, and was responsible for expanding local services. Tom speaks affectionately of his father, often drawing out a certificate signed by the Premier of Ontario indicating that a township had been named after his father. His mother's side of the family was an even greater reason for Tom's local status. Tom's great-grandfather was a chief who signed Treaty 9 for the Fort Hope band in 1905, and his uncle was a successful competitor of the Fort Hope HBC store. Since most of the Collins population is composed of transplanted Fort Hopers, Tom's family connections validate his claim to the position of leader.

If Tom is the brawn of ORG, then his brother John is the "behind-the-scenes" thinker. John runs the local store and post office, and spends most of his time in Collins while Tom hops from one meeting to another in Thunder Bay and Toronto. John's home is the centre of ORG operations, and it is here that visitors are entertained and the endless discussions of strategy are held. John benefits from the same family connections as his brother, and from an early age learned about operating a successful business from his father. His demeanour in dealing with Collins people is more of a joking, jovial sort, a characteristic contrasting with Tom's somewhat petulant nature. John claims to have learned to speak Ojibwa from his wife Ellen, a steady church supporter and local representative of the Ontario Native Women's Association. John is a major source of my information on Collins, and his patient side is revealed by the numerous times that he was willing to sit up all night with me talking about Collins's state of affairs.

A third brother, Allen, completes the triumvirate. Allen is the youngest, in his early thirties, and is much more retiring and introverted than his older brothers. He does, however, make an important contribution to ORG because his time spent in Toronto as a CNR bookkeeper equipped ORG with much-needed accounting skills. When motivated, Allen can show a fierce determination to succeed. For instance, when spring weather threatened to destroy the winter cargo road to the construction site fifty miles away at Whitewater Lake, Allen would make as many as two trips a day lugging a trailer of supplies behind his snowmachine. He would be gone early in the morning and it was not until two or three in the morning that he would return. It was such a precarious journey alone that most of the family waited up for him, crowded around the stove. The door would open and Allen would stumble in, his face and clothing dripping with icicles, his legs so stiffened by the cold that he needed help to walk. You knew that Allen cared about the success of ORG.

Annie, mother of the three brothers, is the resident matriarch of Collins. She lives with sons Allen and Tom, who are bachelors, and frequently chastizes them for their lack of help about the house. Annie is a steadfast person who has been able to survive two heart attacks with enough strength to do the laundry outdoors. There is no doubt that Annie was a major contributor to the success of her husband's fur trading operations at thirteen different posts in northern Ontario, where she conducted the behind-the-counter operations and acted as all-around translator of Indian life. For her three sons, Annie is living proof of their claim to elite status in the Indian community.

Aside from the McTavish family, Joe Tobano, a treaty Indian, has considerable influence in the Collins community. Joe is the CNR section foreman, and therefore controls one of the few local sources of full-time employment. Joe is also one of the most prolific trappers in the village, as he consistently sells more furs to the store each year than anyone else. His long time service with the railway has given him enough cash so that he can afford the best hunting and fishing equipment (snowmachines, rifles, boats) which lessens his dependence on store-bought foods. His family, comprising six children (four of whom are adopted), are often taken on these bush trips. Joe's position as a local leader is strengthened by his affinal link to the McTavish family (his wife is the sister of Ellen McTavish, John McTavish's wife), and by his ability to excel in the two main sectors of the Collins economy—wage work and subsistence production.

Robert Potan, Ellen's cousin, is an important authority figure in Collins because he is the main ORG foreman. Heavy set and powerfully built, Robert is widely known for his expertise in the bush, and the men at the Whitewater have a healthy respect for him. He also worked for the railway for a while as a section foreman, until deciding to quit and devote his energy to trapping and hunting. Robert's brother-in-law, Steve Wabens, has a similar life style. Steve usually spends the winter with his family running a trap line and acting as caretaker of the tourist lodge at Whitewater Lake. In the summer Steve and Robert organize the men for ORG's various bush projects, and for this reason they are the main links between ORG's administrators (the McTavish brothers, who do not spend much time in the bush) and Collins's workers.

Characteristics of Leadership Elite

Collins leaders share three main characteristics—similar incomes, age, and family ties. Leaders have much higher incomes than other members of the community. The six male leaders discussed above had an average (earned) income of $7,900 in 1974. This figure contrasts with the sum of $3,600, the average income per worker in Collins's forty-four-member labour force. The leaders, then, make more than twice as much as the average worker.

A second characteristic is that the leaders are all within the same age group (in their twenties and thirties). For the most part they are also old friends who shared in teenage exploits, and all are considered to be members of the same (Fort Hope) band. The McTavishes are considered to be Métis by the larger society, but in Collins they are regarded as Fort Hope people, members of the same band as their treaty counterparts. The reasons for this are that all of the McTavishes were born in Fort Hope and are related to other Fort Hope people through ties of marriage and blood. These kinship links are the third main feature of the Collins leadership group (Figure 7).

At first one is tempted to suggest that political relations in Collins have been modeled on kin ties. The argument would go like this: in small societies kin ties, or the organization of these ties, provide a model through which an aspiring individual could pattern transactional relationships with potential followers. One reason why this could occur is that the costs of attracting a group of followers would be low among kinsfolk but higher if the leader had to negotiate new transactions or other alliances with non-relatives. The problem with this explanation is that if we assume a close parallel between patterns of kinship on the one hand, and patterns of political organization on the other, then we would be pushed to ask about the conditions that must exist for this relationship to develop.

FIGURE 7

Kinship Ties among Collins Leaders

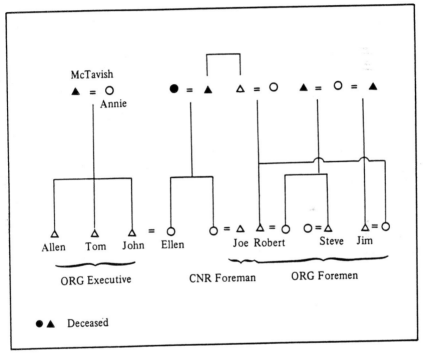

A second way of looking at it is that the interpersonal alliances came first, and the kin ties later. Starting with the observation that many of the crucial kin ties connecting leaders are affinal ones (in Figure 7), we would indicate that leaders were united by bonds of friendship and band membership long before they were married. Marriage, therefore, was preceded by long-established partnerships among men for whom marriage was a formalization or explicit recognition of pre-existing ties. This process can be illustrated by an examination of how these kin ties were built up over time. Referring again to Figure 7, the first marriages were by John McTavish and Joe Tobano, who married sisters. Next, the sister's patrilateral parallel-cousin, Robert Potan, married a friend's (Steve Wabens') sister. In turn, Steve's half-brother, Jim Moose, married Robert Potan's sister. The result is a closely knit group which evolved by boyhood friends marrying each other's sisters, and if not their sisters, they married their friend's cousins. In fact, these are traditional means of establishing wider alliances among northern Ojibwa (cf. Landes 1937: 18-30; Rogers 1962: B47-B50).

ORG and the CNR

There are two principal employers in Collins—ORG and the CNR. If we examine the structure and composition of these organizations, along with their role or function in the community, we are able to see reasons why some groups should be stronger than others or why some leaders attract more followers than others. Actually the word "group" in the Collins case is somewhat misleading since there are important differences between the ORG and CNR "groups" which restrict the ways of comparing them. The CNR crew, for example, is a group to the extent that its members earn a living together and often form friendships among fellow employees. But the CNR crew, unlike ORG, lacks organizational goals. The CNR foreman is himself an employee of an outside organization, rather than a self-recruited entrepreneur as are the ORG leaders. When one compares the roles of leaders in ORG (dealing with outside authorities, generating and dispensing jobs, or acting as local patrons) with those in the CNR, it is difficult to represent the CNR foreman as a similar "leader." Aside from jobs on the railway, the foreman has few benefits to distribute. His income and hunting success place him among the elite, but his leadership role in the community is restricted by the few resources at his disposal. Both ORG and the CNR are "groups," but of a different order.

A more precise picture of differences in group composition emerge when we examine specific interpersonal ties. My assumption here is that a group with a denser network of ties among its members could be considered a more cohesive group than one with more limited, single-stranded relationships. Seven major relationships utilized in this discussion are as follows:

(1) primary kinship relationships, that is, members of the same family;

(2) secondary kinship relationships, that is, people related through second generation and affinal links;

(3) friendship links;

(4) economic exchange involving horizontal relationships in terms of input over a long period of time, such as may exist between neighbouring households, or between those in a hunting or trapping partnership;

(5) patron-client relations with a vertical economic and social base, such as the fur trader/trapper relationship;

(6) transactional relationships which occur at only one particular point in time, such as providing bail money or a job;

(7) same band membership.

These criteria are then listed horizontally, by number, and members of both ORG and CNR groups are listed vertically (Table 15). Using this format, a leader's links with other group members are displayed.

TABLE 15

Recruitment Criteria, ORG and CNR Groups

	Criteria						
	1	2	3	4	5	6	7
ORG Group							
John McTavish's links with							
T. McTavish	*				*		*
A. McTavish	*				*		*
R. Potan		*	*	*		*	*
J. Moose		*	*	*		*	*
S. Wabens			*		*	*	*
Totals	2	2	3	2	3	3	5 (20)
CNR Group							
J. Tobano's links with							
P. Kwissis			*			*	
E. Kwissis						*	
R. Birch						*	*
J. Otter			*			*	*
E. Crane			*			*	*
J. Bouchard						*	
Totals	—	—	3	—	—	6	3 (12)

The most obvious fact revealed by the chart is that the ORG group has utilized far more diverse internal linkages than the CNR group. ORG has recruited kinsfolk, friends, and those with the same band affiliation. On-going patron/client relationships are used in conjunction with more specific transactional relationships, such as providing jobs for followers. In contrast to ORG, the CNR group uses far fewer and more circumscribed links among group members. Kin are not recruited, nor are long term patron/client relationships utilized. The main mode of recruitment is the single-stranded transactional relationship involving the hiring of workers by the section foreman. Sometimes friendship links are developed after a worker is hired, but friendship is not an important factor in recruitment, as is the case with ORG members.

ORG and the CNR provide Collins with a dualistic structure, mainly because cash enters the Collins economy from two divergent outside sources. One source is what may be termed the "private sphere," that is, benefits dispensed by the CNR . The other is the "public sphere" comprising resources available from various government agencies upon which the ORG group depends. In Collins these private and public spheres are virtually discrete since there are basic differences in the organization of work, in the duration of projects, and in worker's perceptions of various benefits and disadvantages of CNR work as opposed to ORG activities. But the interesting point is that activities in each of the CNR and ORG spheres tend to reflect somewhat of a mirror image of the other—for each disadvantage that workers perceive in the CNR sphere there is a corresponding advantage available in the ORG sphere, such as high geographical mobility for railway work and low mobility requirements for ORG activities, or full-time versus part-time employment. The effect of such phenomena is that these two spheres of activity tend to complement each other. This concept of complementary spheres can be a useful analytical tool in illustrating the processes of sub-group interaction in small communities such as Collins. From this perspective we can see the emergence of ORG as a spin-off or complement to CNR activities, where the former offers advantages by building on the disadvantages of association with the latter.

For many settlements in northern Ontario the railway has been the only source of perdurable, full-time employment that Indian workers have been able to secure. Wages for railway employment are usually as high as that received for equivalent work in the south, a situation which contrasts with the minimum wages that native workers often receive from other employment sources in northern areas. The railway also allows for a reduction in transportation costs, since railway employees and their families can travel free of charge along the route of their own section. Housing expenses are another area where costs are reduced, since the CNR maintains three or four small cottages for the accommodation of employees at each section. Despite these benefits, railway workers must also take into consideration the drawbacks associated with CNR work.

Automation and new automotive machinery have meant a reduction in available jobs on the CNR. Many sections along the line have been eliminated, and the size of section crews has dwindled. An added complaint is that management frequently transfers workers from one section to another as labour requirements fluctuate, and this has had disruptive effects on workers' community and family life. A related point is that full-time employment has an effect on peoples' ability to secure subsistence resources, because it restricts the amount of time that they can spend away from the village hunting and fishing. Most railway workers, though, arrange to take their vacations or leaves of absence during those periods of the year when fish and game are most abundant.

The complementary nature of costs and benefits between the private (CNR) and public (ORG) spheres of the Collins community can now be delineated more precisely. In essence, benefits which are perceived by workers for the public sphere are seen as disadvantages in the private sphere, and vice versa, such that ORG emerges as a complement of the CNR. For example, a primary advantage of working for ORG is that there is more potential for growth in ORG employment than now exists with the CNR, coupled with a greater potential for local advancement in ORG supervisory positions. Collins workers also indicate that they found ORG employment satisfying because it takes place in a bush environment—work based on traditional know-how and forest lore—than is the case with railway work which has become highly mechanized. ORG was attractive to others because it is based primarily on the tourist trade where outsiders are dependent upon local people, whereas in the railway-work environment Indian workers often feel subservient to whites.

This reversal in dependency patterns is further found in the local belief that ORG allows for more autonomy in economic decision making than is the case with Eurocanadian work organizations which dictate decisions from the outside, such as worker transfers, employment quotas, and wage rates. Similarly, treaty Indians in Collins remember that on a reserve the Indian agent has the prerogative of forwarding decisions directly to his superiors in the Indian Affairs Branch without prior consultation with local band councils. Yet there is one drawback for local autonomy-seeking organizations such as ORG in that there exists some confusion in role expectations resulting from the fact that the ORG leaders maintain less ordered relations with outside authorities. In contrast with other organizations, such as the Indian Affairs Branch structure in which role performance has become highly formalized, ORG/outside interaction is less predictable than would be the case with a more established organization. Actually, ORG has adopted a strategy such that outside agents would have difficulty in predicting the future actions of ORG. The purpose of this strategy was to perpetuate negotiations with external agencies in the hope that such a strategy would lead to an increased flow of resources to the local level and, incidently, for more powerful local leaders.

In sum, when resources enter a small community from both "private" and "public" sectors of a larger, encapsulating society one can expect the emergence of dual organizations at the local level, such that the second group will emerge as a complement of the first, based on local perceptions of potential costs and benefits of membership in both groups. This is an important process in the shaping of leader/follower relations in the Collins community. The next section discusses the strategies that the trader's sons use for political gain in their role as local businessmen, aside from their role as ORG executives.

Business Opportunity and Political Strategy

There has really been only one "business" in Collins—the trading store complex—and while it has assumed various forms over the last sixty years, its longevity can be attributed to a sharp business acumen and a recognition of political realities by its owners. The fact that any business has been able to remain solvent for so long, by northern standards, in competition with such conglomerates as the HBC and mail-order companies would make it worthy of special note in its own right despite the store's small, usually poor clientele. Why should a merchant continue to operate under conditions where stock turnover is low, indebted customers the rule, and where profits have been minimal for many years?

Collins people say that up until 1960, when the fur trade was still a viable enterprise, trading stores along the rail line were stocked with a greater variety of goods than is the case today. Previously, consumer demands could all be satisfied at one location, but today only food and some equipment are purchased in Collins. The big mail-order houses are relied upon for most other items, especially clothing and household supplies. Outside businesses cater to a much larger consumer population than can be found locally, and for this reason they can more easily meet consumer expectations. With this trend towards outside purchasing, a local business with a limited clientele is likely to stagnate.

Along with a low sales volume and a diminishing ability to turn over a profit, local operators are also likely to encounter other problems. Accounting practices and credit arrangements, for example, are different today than in the past. Until a few decades ago stock replacement could be balanced against fur returns, as stock inventory fluctuated with the credit that was extended in the previous year. With the decline in fur trading, store owners in northern areas were often reduced to dispensers of welfare vouchers for government agencies. In this case the same accounting principle applied as before, except that vouchers instead of furs were traded for the store's stock. But a welfare economy is essentially a closed system since almost nobody has "surplus" income, and for this reason there is little opportunity for business expansion.

Today the general store in Collins survives less as a business where regular profits can be expected, than as a community service for a political following. Credit in varying degrees is extended to virtually every adult in the community, even though the past performance of some customers would seem to necessitate a termination of credit. Actually the most perplexing anomaly for local merchants is that many customers endeavour to maintain a good credit standing in nearby settlements where the variety and quantity of merchandise is relatively extensive, but where credit will be terminated for non-payment of past-due accounts. In Collins, bills at the store are allowed to accumulate for long periods with only intermittent, token payments. But everyone realizes that the store owner in Collins is unlikely to curtail anyone's credit, and that he can be expected to distribute food in hard times regardless of a debtor's negligence.

For the store owner who is also a political leader, it is not surprising that many members of the community are indebted to him for various reasons. A leader in this circumstance attempts to avoid role conflicts by neglecting to pursue a rigorous policy of repayment on overdue accounts. He prefers to be rich in followers, rather than in monetary terms. The drawback is that because of a leader's multiplicity of roles, followers tend to expect him to distribute the resources at his disposal in times of need. This expectation on the part of followers who are also business customers causes a conflict with any orientation towards business profit that the store owner may have. By acquiescing in these expectations the leader/owner maximizes social, rather than material ends—store goods and credit are exchanges for future compliance in other areas.

For business operators in small communities who are not also political leaders, the consequences of policies that run contrary to local expectations can be ruinous. By attempting to further material ends, while simultaneously holding the line on credit advances, a business will probably lose customers to other entrepreneurs more willing to sacrifice material rewards for other considerations, such as prestige or status. And further, community fission could result when entrepreneurs from different settlements are simultaneously attempting to attract customers and followers. A hard-nosed businessman in this situation flirts with bankruptcy.

Actually this situation did occur in a settlement just forty miles from Collins. At Allenwater Bridge the trading store, an HBC operation, remained a viable business enterprise during the fur trade era because it followed the accepted practice of extending to trappers a credit equivalent to the value of their previous winter's catch. But when transfer payments proliferated during the decline of trapping in the 1950s, residents of Allenwater adopted an enterprising strategy whereby they could maximize their intake of consumer goods while minimizing their cash outflow. They were able to accomplish this contradictory state of affairs by compounding their credit arrangements, first at the local store in Allenwater, and then at the stores in other settlements along the rail line. It was because of an over-extension of credit in an attempt to attract new customers, and an inability to settle overdue accounts, that the store business in Allen-water suffered financial ruin. The store operator was not able to translate financial debts into political allegiance—community fragmentation, rather than consolidation, was the result. Within a decade Allen-water's population dropped from two hundred people to a couple of families, and the store operator moved to Sioux Lookout.

The Allenwater business was an outside institution existing for the sole purpose of making profit, and therefore contrasts with the multi-plex nature of the Collins operation. The Collins store owner was able to keep debts within acceptable bounds by restricting the variety and quantity of goods offered for sale. And with the increased cash flow resulting from the leaders' creation of new job opportunities, such as the construction of the Whitewater tourist operation, sales at the Collins store now yield enough of a monetary return to keep the business solvent, but without eradicating entirely the indebtedness of client-followers.

In all, a main problem for leaders in Collins is how to organize available cash, labour and environmental resources, while at the same time maintaining the support of community members. In his role as ORG co-ordinator and store operator, John McTavish has chosen to forgo material profit in order to stabilize a following based on in-debtedness relationships and increased community services. In essence, such strategies which aim to attract a following or otherwise gain further support are a matter of recruitment. We can now consider strategies aimed at the preservation of this support, which is a matter of group maintenance.

Maintaining Group Boundaries

Much of the success of the trader's three sons can be attributed to their role as middlemen between the local native population and external authorities. Such a position allows leaders to function as a boundary maintenance mechanism, helping to preserve and protect the differences of the local subsystem. When actions are taken which serve to insulate local people from external influence, the dependency of local people on their leaders is increased. Such actions circumvent the emergence of opposing middlemen, and restrict the wider dissemination of knowledge and skills which make the rise of competing leaders possible.

The example chosen to illustrate this boundary maintenance theme centres about an attempt by the Ontario government to integrate the Collins settlement, and others like Collins which the government erroneously referred to as "unorganized communities," into Ontario's system of municipal government. The government argued that unorganized communities, because of their small populations, could not be incorporated and were therefore missing out on basic government services. In order to receive these services all the people had to do was accept certain government guidelines, such as the holding of regular elections to fill positions designated by the government. Despite a promise of increased local services, the trader's sons fought against incorporation into the wider municipal structure because they believed that such a move would undermine local autonomy in decision making.

As far as officials in the Ontario government were concerned, some form of "legally recognized" municipal organization was a necessary prerequisite for the provision of basic social and physical services. To this end the government proposed to integrate the hundred or so rural communities in northern Ontario which lacked elective government into the present municipal system for purposes of taxation and the establishment of elected community councils. The government promoted the bill (Bill 102, or The Northern Communities Act) by emphasizing increased local services (electrical power, running water, sewage disposal) which the government suggested would become available to unorganized communities in the event that the bill became law.

When I first discussed the government's proposal with ORG's main leaders, Tom and John McTavish, they were enthusiastic about the prospect of receiving additional government aid with no added cost. "After all," said John, "what do we have to lose? If the government wants to increase its help, then we should give them the opportunity to do it." After about a week their opinions began to change as they thought about the wider implications of the government's proposal, as indicated by Tom's statement that "What does the government mean that it needs 'official mechanisms' to implement basic services.

The Ministry of the Environment built our wells [in 1972] didn't they, and without 'official' channels. Anyway we would never have the tax base for such grand schemes. You can't expect the government to give us these services for nothing." John interrupted at this point, "You know it looks to me like the government is just trying to control every little area where right now it doesn't have much influence. If we go along with this we're going to have people like [he names a person with low community status] running things, and that will be the end of ORG."

This discussion indicates that ORG leaders objected to government attempts to create local bureaucratic links through elected community councils, which the government would ultimately control through provincial statute. The key to the community council idea is the government strategy to create a structure capable of delivering the maximum possible service at the lowest administrative cost and, at the same time, to exploit the democratic advantage of small size. The trader's sons felt that the proposed legislation would give the provincial government a greater measure of control in local affairs than currently exists in most isolated northern communities, a process which they saw as threatening to their positions as local leaders.

In sum, the discussion thus far illustrates that the development of ORG was made possible by two factors. The first factor was that the trader-patron, because of economic circumstances, chose to diversify his relations with followers in an attempt to prevent the fragmentation or dispersion of his clientage. In order to circumvent this dispersion, single-stranded relations built up during the fur trade were expanded to multi-stranded relations involving wage work and a variety of other services. The trader also pursued outside agents in an attempt to secure support from the larger society in solving local problems. The second factor was that the trader's sons were able to build on their father's gains and, in turn, to forge a corporate identity for the local political structure. Thus, ORG was ensured by this tactic of securing a wider basis of local support than would have been possible under the trader's more individualistic style of leadership. Further activity, such as ORG's opposition to the government's unorganized communities proposal, served to maintain ORG's local influence.

ORG Development Strategy

Ogoki River Guides Ltd. was incorporated as a non-profit native corporation, as the executive put it, "dedicated to the social and economic improvement of all Collins people." Actually their motives were not entirely altruistic given the fact that the permanent core of the corporation consists of brothers who also operate a retail outlet in

Collins, and a kinsman who has long been the CNR section foreman — positions which depend on the continued existence of Collins as a stable, economically viable community both as a source of labour and new cash flow. Any future projects which served to increase employment in the Collins area would therefore benefit leaders and followers alike.

The high unemployment in the community assured a readily available supply of labour, and the mounting social problems associated with backwoods poverty provided ample opportunities for government involvement. All that was needed was a linkage mechanism, someone with the capabilities to translate the inaccessible and unfamiliar into the possible and known. Given the background of their father, the brothers were able to make a good start in achieving this objective. As teenagers they had helped their father operate a fishing and hunting lodge at Mud River, and later participated in the operation of their father's restaurant in Armstrong. By the time the brothers were young men they had become familiar with many facets of the tourist trade—advertising, scheduling of arrivals and departures, hiring guides and cooks, customer relations, ordering food and other supplies, accounting practices, transportation, determining the best sites, and so on. Given the availability of efficient guides and attractive natural resources in the Collins area, the brothers consulted with other members of the community and came to the conclusion that a large-scale tourist operation offered the best hope for vitalizing the Collins economy. The president of ORG, Tom McTavish, summed up the situation by stating, "Essentially what we want to do is industrialize this area, but in a way that fits in with our way of life and doesn't destroy the environment. We've got the human resources and fantastic natural resources up here, all we need is help from the government to get us going."

With this objective in the forefront, Collins leaders launched an active campaign in an effort to solicit support. The eldest brother, as president of ORG, approached numerous government agencies both in Thunder Bay and Toronto, while another brother, the secretary-treasurer, stayed in Collins entertaining outside officials and initiating correspondence by mail and telephone. Matters relating to employment were discussed with Manpower officials and the Dean of Retraining at Confederation College. Aspects of the tourist trade were considered with representatives of the Ministry of Industry and Tourism, the Ministry of Natural Resources, and the manager of Domtar's woodlands operations. Technical and marketing consultants of the Northern Ontario Development Corporation were visited. Problems of housing construction and maintenance in the North were considered with members of the Ontario Housing Corporation. Social problems relating to long-term unemployment were discussed with representatives of the Ministry of Community and Social Services. In addition, Collins leaders sought the help of opposition party members in an effort to gain support for their ventures in the provincial legislature. They were also able to cultivate support from the news media, locally and in the provincial capital (articles on Collins have appeared in the *Globe and Mail*).

As an initial or trial project (in 1972), the corporation undertook to build an experimental log house in an attempt to demonstrate ways of providing inexpensive and sturdy accommodations for people living in subarctic conditions. An additional aim was to show that the use of local labour and forest products could produce acceptable housing at low cost. A provincial government body, the Ontario Housing Corporation, provided technical advice on the project, and a grant of $4,000 from the Indian Community Branch defrayed the cost of materials not locally available (such as interior finishing, roofing, plumbing, and fixtures).

From 1972 to the present, the major objective of ORG has been the development of a community-operated tourist industry, and all subsequent projects have been geared towards this end. Collins people were quick to realize the social and economic importance of the project. As Tom McTavish phrased it, "What we're talking about here is the survival of a community. If we fail to make a go of this project the people will turn to welfare, and Collins will become just another dying Indian community." As indicated earlier, Collins leaders have long been aware of the potential for developing the tourist industry in the North. Several mobile tourist camps have successfully functioned in the Collins area, and the general consensus was that there were sufficient market possibilities for additional operations. In the past, native people have guided for white entrepreneurs, but now feel that they have the expertise to initiate their own operations. The stumbling block to this end has been a shortage of investment capital, which is a characteristic shared by most northern native settlements. From the native perspective, the government has been ready to invest in social welfare schemes, but has placed a low priority on investment for economic development purposes.

As a preparatory phase for their tourist lodge endeavour, ORG approached officials in the Ministry of Natural Resources so that a lake management and shoreline survey could be conducted in the Whitewater Lake area. A number of Collins people were hired to assist in the survey work, and equipment, such as boats and motors, was rented from ORG. Next, an Opportunities for Youth grant allowed for the hiring of fifteen men to organize canoe routes, to cut portages, and to clean up camp sites in the area. Still in 1972, a Local Initiatives Program grant was utilized to construct snowmobile trails which were later used as winter roads on which cargo was hauled to the Whitewater site. This preliminary phase of grantmanship concluded with a provincial grant, from the Indian Community Branch, of $7,000 for the purchase of freighter canoes and motors. Revenue derived from rental of this equipment (for the survey work mentioned above) was subsequently used to reduce costs involved in various community recreation projects, such as the construction of a skating rink in Collins.

Finally, in the spring of 1974 the Department of Regional Economic Expansion (DREE) and the Agricultural Rehabilitation and Development Agency (ARDA) issued a joint press release announcing that a grant of $325,000 had been awarded to ORG for the construction of a wilderness lodge at Whitewater Lake. It is interesting to note in this regard that the Federal Minister of DREE explained that the DREE-ARDA grant had been made possible by a new, broadened interpretation of the DREE-ARDA agreement. This new interpretation allowed, for the first time in Ontario, a non-profit corporation to represent a rural population of native extraction where no legal municipal structure exists to take advantage of the DREE-ARDA agreement.

As a compliment to this discussion of local economic strategy, it is important to indicate that government funding agencies have different organizational objectives and, as such, their effects on community development also tend to vary. The Indian Community Branch, for example, has a relatively small budget, just $1.3 million for the 1972-73 fiscal year. This organization provides what may be termed "seed money" as an impetus for community members to initiate projects themselves. If these projects have potential or long-term implications, the Indian Community Branch encourages local leaders to look elsewhere for more extensive funding. The Branch's primary goal is to assist both status and non-status Indian communities in, as outlined in their brochure, "the process of self-determination and self-development—to assist community leaders to take charge of their own affairs." In all, funding from the ICB provides a good basis for initiating projects, and for providing auxiliary funds for larger projects. In Collins the ICB funded two operations subsidiary to the wilderness lodge program: boat and motor purchases (1972) and a guiding course (1973). It also provided seed money for the experimental housing project mentioned above.

Two Federal Government agencies—Opportunities for Youth (Secretary of State Department) and the Local Initiative Program (Manpower and Immigration)—provided funding for the explicit purpose of raising the level of employment in Canada. These programs were essentially stop-gap measures in that the primary objective was to provide short-term employment in the so-called depressed regions of the country. Officials in these agencies would have preferred that the total amount of funding go directly to wages, although the usual practice was to allow about 20 percent of the grant for capital expenditures. They made it quite clear that if this 20 percent ceiling was exceeded, a project was liable to be cancelled. But here again, these sources of funding could be usefully employed in the aid of a larger project, especially at times when funding for the larger endeavour needed to be diverted from wages to capital expenditures. In Collins, OFY and LIP funds were employed in this manner to construct snow-mobile cargo roads to Whitewater Lake (1972, 1974), to clear portages (1972), to promote recreational activities (1973), and to investigate the market potential for Indian crafts and building methods (1974-75).

A primary source of funding for large projects, ones which promise to yield long-term employment possibilities is the ARDA branch of the Ontario Ministry of Agriculture and Food. The total allotment available to the Province of Ontario for the term of the cost-sharing agreement between the Province and the Government of Canada is not less than $30 million (*Federal-Provincial Rural Development Agreement, 1970-1975*). For non-reserve Indian communities such as Collins, a notable part of this agreement (section 12) states that: "Ontario may apply ARDA programs to Indian lands and Indian people. In the event that Indians are involved in a program Canada will negotiate special cost-sharing arrangements to the extent that Indians are involved." This section of the agreement has been a special source of frustration for Collins leaders because of its lack of specificity — it does not specify whether the paragraph refers to treaty Indians, that is Indians registered under the Indian Act, to non-status Indians, or to both.

Treaty Indians are a federal responsibility, and for this reason Ontario can be expected to argue that it should not be burdened with Indian Affairs Branch responsibilities. This is another example of that nebulous area which non-status and off-reserve Indians occupy with respect to provincial/federal responsibilities. This point is especially interesting in light of the fact that the Ontario-Canada ARDA agreement is phrased in the usual legal argot in which a concerted effort was made to carefully define such terms as "sharable cost," "selected rural areas," "projects," and so on. But the issue as to which Indians, i.e., status or non-status, the agreement refers to was effectively skirted by the use of such ambiguous terms as "Indian lands" and "Indian people."

Since mid-1972 ARDA officials had maintained that they could not consider funding the wilderness lodge project because ORG was not deemed, by the provincial government, to be a public body. By ARDA's definition a "public body" is one having a legal municipal political structure with elected representatives, and therefore the Collins project should be disqualified because ORG did not, in their opinion, meet these requirements. In rebuttal, Collins leaders maintained that the Collins community was clearly populated by "Indians" and, given this fact, the tourist project should be considered on its merits alone, rather than on extraneous interpretations of the ARDA agreement. The leaders also indicated, to paraphrase their comments, that ARDA grants for the construction of tourist facilities had been made in the past to both Indians and non-Indians in Ontario, and the fact that Collins does not have an elected band council, which is only required by reserve communities, should not be the underlying reason for the project's disqualification. But after a lengthy dispute, both DREE and ARDA officials agreed to interpret the clause in the agreement about "Indians" to cover those native people living both on and off reserves.

ORG's endeavours marked the first time that wage labour was available locally from Indian sources, and indeed from any source, aside from short term work for the store owner, guiding for white tourist operators, or jobs provided by the CNR. ORG projects illustrate the priorities placed on wage labour, both by local leaders and outside granting agencies. Presumably both leaders at the local level and those in government tend to judge the success of their efforts by the number of jobs produced. Because of this strategy, a low priority is placed on expenditures for capital equipment and it is for this reason that funds are commonly diverted from one project to another in order to avoid surpassing allowable ceilings placed by granting agencies. More importantly though, this discussion allows one to see the interrelationships among various projects, and the organizational requirements for attaining future goals. By interrelating various work projects, leaders can hope for a more unified work force and thus for a more unified basis for local support.

Two projects in 1972 provided employment for six months, from February to the end of August (Table 16). The first was financed by the Federal Department of Manpower under its Local Initiatives Program. Besides providing immediate wage labour ($100 per week for 250 man-weeks), a major goal was the development of a winter transportation system linking the surrounding communities of Armstrong and Allenwater Bridge. However, the trails were seldom used partly because of the initial capital outlay and expense of snowmobile operation, but also because of the less expensive transportation provided by the CNR. Despite these shortcomings, a stretch of the trail was later used as a winter road for transporting equipment to the lodge site at

Whitewater Lake, and thereby allowed for a reduction in air transportation costs the following summer. When the spring break-up was complete, fifteen persons were employed under an Opportunities for Youth grant to cut portages and clear campsites on the canoe route to Whitewater, a route seldom used since the trapping days. In all, approximately 150 worker-weeks of wage labour were provided by this endeavour.

An example of the way in which local people were quick to capitalize on new opportunities is evident when a provincial agency, the Indian Community Branch, awarded a grant of $7,000 in 1972 for the purchase of boats and motors for the operation of the tourist lodge. Then, when the Ministry of Natural Resources expressed a desire to rent the boats for their lake management programs, local leaders convinced the officials to hire Collins people to operate them. In addition, money from renting the equipment to the Ministry (about $900) was then used during the following winter for recreational activities (a new hockey rink). These activities were funded by an Opportunities for Youth grant, and the rental revenue was spent on building materials and snow removal equipment, purchases which were not allowed under the granting agency's conditions. In all, twenty-nine men and women were employed (at $90 per week) resulting in about $13,000 in wages for Collins workers (140 worker-weeks).

TABLE 16

Projects of Ogoki River Guides Ltd., 1971-75

| Year | Expenditures | | Workers employed | Worker-weeks employment |
	Wages	Equipment		
1971	—	650	—	—
1972	39,300	17,550	42	400
1973	20,200	500	43	220
1974	121,500	201,300	83	840
1975[a]	19,900	3,800	16	173
Totals	$200,900	$223,800	184	1,633

[a] The figures for 1975 represent only a partial listing for that year. Total expenditures, including wages and equipment, amounted to $290,000.

Another step in the overall plan to establish a locally-based tourist industry came during the next summer (1973) when Confederation College of Thunder Bay provided an $8,000 guide training course for fourteen young men, taught by an Ojibwa guide from the Albany River (the emphasis was less on hunting and fishing skills than on customer relations). The course was quick to pay dividends for those enrolled. Some of the fourteen had guided in 1972 for white operators at $20 a day, but in 1973, all of those in the course had been hired as moose-hunting guides at $30 a day. As John MacTavish put it, "the guides are simply more valuable to the lodge owners now and they are willing to pay." Incidentally, this guiding course program is a significant departure from the routine procedure of teaching skills appropriate for relocation to large urban centres.

In economic terms, 1974 was a productive year as Collins projects contributed over $120,000 in wages to the area economy. Another LIP grant was alloted to complete forty-five miles of winter cargo road to Whitewater, and twenty-three workers earned $22,000, which accounted for 215 worker-weeks of employment. During the summer months the long-awaited ARDA grant allowed for a start on the construction of the tourist facilities at Whitewater. For the first time, workers from other communities were hired to supplement the Collins work force—Collins men earning $57,000 in wages, while those from elsewhere made $43,000. The wage rate was now up to $3.40 per hour, compared with $2.25 an hour for previous projects, and 670 worker-weeks employment were generated by this start on the lodge venture. In addition, $170,000 was spent on capital expenditures, a significant departure from all previous work programs where capital expenses were restricted to only 20 percent of the total grant. The following winter (1974-75) another LIP grant was used to hire twelve Collins workers (for 173 worker-weeks) in a training program to explore marketing possibilities for Indian crafts and building methods.

Conclusion

This chapter contains a review of the major developments in Collins's political organization over the last thirty years. The main purpose of this review has been to isolate the strategies leaders have used to hold the Collins population together, to gain local support, and to obtain benefits for followers.

The discussion began with an examination of the role of the Collins "trader-patron" during the 1950s. This was a period when Collins economic difficulties posed a serious problem for the community. Indeed, they threatened the settlement's very existence. Fur prices were steadily declining and there was a general trend away from life in the bush. The trading post, school, and churches in Collins provided a focus for permanent settlement, but there was little in the way of new economic alternatives to trapping for the population.

Railway work had provided the main access to wage labour, but automation, diesel engines, and new maintenance programs caused a sharp reduction in the CNR's labour requirements. The local fur trader saw these trends as a serious threat to his livelihood and, as a consequence, took definite steps to counteract declining incomes and employment opportunities. He realized that it was imperative that he put new benefits in the hands of Collins residents or they would simply move elsewhere. To this end the trader made a start towards providing part-time employment, increasing local services, and cultivating associations with agents of the outside society.

With their father's death in the 1960s, the trader's three sons built on his political foundation. They secured the active participation of a few close friends and kinsfolk from the Fort Hope group to form a leadership core. At first this core group formed a "Committee for Development" in Collins as an attempt to mobilize the trader's outside contacts, and to gain practical knowledge about bureaucratic techniques for obtaining benefits. After this "practice session," the fully chartered corporation of Ogoki River Guides Ltd. was formed in order to tackle Collins's pressing economic problems.

ORG has emerged as the "legal" vehicle through which government officials have begun to deal with the Collins community in the absence of a legally organized council, and has provided the administrative framework necessary for the integration of diverse work projects. The organization's main strategy for obtaining outside benefits has been termed "grantmanship," that is, making attempts to develop local employment opportunities with the aid of government investment. The "non-profit" orientation of ORG is a reflection of the importance placed on locally-controlled operations, and this is partly the reason why success tends to be judged primarily by the number of jobs produced. Because of this perception of success, leaders' rise to positions of power in small communities can be measured by their ability to generate remunerative and service-related benefits for followers. Thus, a rise in worker-weeks of wage employment is an important indicator of a leaders' expanding sphere of local influence.

This expanding influence is demonstrated by the impact on the Collins work force of ORG attempts to dispense economic benefits. The principle question here is how many Collins people were able to secure ORG jobs, and for how long? For example, for the three year period from 1972 to 1974, 184 workers earned $200,806 during 101 weeks, for a total of 1,633 worker-weeks of employment. Each person then earned $1,091 and worked for 8.9 weeks, on the average. On a yearly basis, about 544 worker-weeks employment were available and 61 people were hired. What does all of this tell us about ORG strategy in distributing benefits to followers?

The most important consideration is that 544 worker-weeks employment can be allocated in various ways. The same employment total, for instance, can be used to hire 11 people on a full-time basis for one year, or 22 at half-time, and so on. In Collins, ORG hired about 60 people on average per year (for about 9 weeks each). Given the option of giving a lot of work to a few people, or, alternatively, giving a little work to many people, it is evident that ORG leaders have opted for the latter approach. This suggests that in areas of high unemployment leaders attempt to initiate projects which bridge employment gaps between times when work is more readily available. Such a strategy allows for a maximum spread of earnings over the entire community, which in the process increases leaders' support among more "peripheral" followers. By giving a little to just about everyone, leaders lessen the risk of alienating a large portion of their following, which is a probable consequence if a few men were hired for the whole year while many other men remained idle. Such a "spreading the wealth" tactic, then, allows for a wide base of local support through the judicious allocation of available resources. It also allows for satisfaction of the cultural norm of generosity, a characteristic traditionally expected of Indian leaders.

CHAPTER FIVE

ORG and the Whitewater Project

ORG's negotiations with government officials over funding for the wilderness lodge at Whitewater Lake seemed to take so long that when the money was actually awarded it came as somewhat of a shock, especially to the McTavish brothers. For two years or more they had been shuttling back and forth between Collins, Thunder Bay, and Toronto, meeting with MPs and numerous government representatives, and spending endless hours on the telephone. Now all of this had changed. There was no more need for extensive negotiations on the outside; they now had to start thinking seriously about building the lodge, wondering all along if it was really possible. A whole new set of skills were required. The business suits were packed away, and what was happening in Collins was given all the attention. Workers had to be recruited and organized, supplies had to be ordered and equipment made ready. The task was a formidable one and the McTavish brothers attacked it with characteristic vigour.

Construction of the lodge, however, would bring many skilled workers from the outside, and little attention was given, at least in the beginning, to the impact of white workers on the native people of Collins. The fact that the Whitewater site was some fifty miles north of Collins meant that actual contacts were usually only among the Indian and white workers on the construction site. But since the white workers were often filling supervisory roles, there was the important question of control and power between Collins and the outside. Collins people did not want to be swallowed up in a rush of construction activity where it was the whites who made all the important decisions and the Indians who were left to dig the holes and trenches. Collins people hoped that this project would be a chance to learn construction skills that could be applied to future ventures, even if this meant delays in construction schedules and problems with white workers who wanted to leave the bush and its problems as soon as possible.

Leadership and the Supervision of Work

Construction of the tourist lodge at Whitewater Lake began in the spring of 1974. Over the previous winter there had been a lot of discussion between the McTavish brothers, as representatives of ORG, and ARDA officials, who were funding the project, over who should have control over the funds. ORG was eventually given control over most of the money, but it was doled out week-by-week over a three-year period. ARDA personnel reserved the right to hire and pay the construction engineers themselves, which lessened the influence that ORG would be able to exert on the engineers. In their negotiations with ARDA, ORG was able to gain most of the concessions it requested, but its leaders hoped that supervision at the work site would not become a problem.

Two engineers arrived in Collins on schedule. They were greeted at the train by John and Tom McTavish, and then went to John's house where his wife had soup and sandwiches waiting. The engineers explained that they were born in New Zealand, after Tom had asked them about their accents, and that they were brothers. The elder brother, who was in his mid-thirties, was now part owner in a Toronto-based engineering firm and had been hired by ARDA to supervise construction of the Whitewater tourist lodge. He also indicated that he would be able to spend only about two weeks on the construction site, as pressing business awaited him in Toronto. His place on the site itself would be taken by his younger brother, an engineering student in his early twenties. Although they did not say so at the time, I could feel right away that the McTavish brothers were not happy with this arrangement.

The first summer of work, from an ORG perspective, went poorly and was a source of conflict between ORG and the engineers. An example of this involved specially-crafted septic tanks, waiting in Thunder Bay for transport to the construction site at Whitewater Lake, a distance of about two hundred miles. ORG wanted to bring them to the end of the road by truck, and from there carry them to Whitewater by snowmachines (this was in early May when there was still sufficient snow in the bush). The engineers were concerned that the tanks would break over such a rough route, and so they decided to transport them by helicopter, at great expense, to Whitewater Lake. The tanks were subsequently deposited in a bay opposite the site and moored to the dock, but they eventually cracked when the lake froze over during a cold spell. New tanks arrived safely about a month later, but after they were installed it was discovered that part of the system was placed under the site of a planned tennis court, which was against health regulations, and so much of the plumbing had to be dug up.

There were further difficulties which strained the relationship between the younger engineer and the ORG leadership. In the initial stages, bush clearing and site preparation were arduous work and one reason for a high turnover of construction workers during the first summer. ORG leaders then started a recruitment campaign in neighbouring communities but the number of workers on the site was consistently below expected requirements. Long periods of cold, rainy weather frequently stopped work on the tourist lodge and also caused interruptions in the number of flights to Whitewater. With fewer flights, the construction camp suffered shortages in equipment and food, as well as workers. The engineer blamed ORG leaders for these shortages, arguing that it was their responsibility to provide adequate supplies of workers and equipment.

People at the Whitewater camp were also uneasy about the deterioration in camp conditions. Because there were fewer workers than initially anticipated, the younger engineer began pressuring them to work harder and for longer hours. Fewer flights and, as a result, less food available in the camp store, produced more grumbling. Some of the men started to take time off work to go hunting and fishing to augment the camp food supply, a move which further aggravated the engineer. As the search for country food intensified, open arguments between the engineer and the workers became more frequent. As the situation became more difficult it was becoming increasingly obvious that the bush-oriented men of the camp were gaining prominence, much to the detriment of the engineer who saw his authority and influence diminishing on a day-to-day basis. My field notes provide details on some of these emerging conflicts:

August 20, 1974:   Steven and Tommy [two brothers] left early this morning to check the nets they had placed in the narrows. This has been an on-going activity of theirs since my arrival [four days earlier]. Steven is always getting into trouble in the village, but up here at Whitewater he has made a determined effort to organize the men for various bush activities — leading the log-cutting crew during working hours, and taking men to fish at other times. The brothers return about 10 a.m. with a wash tub full of pickerel and sturgeon for the camp kitchen. These fishing trips are becoming more important as they are one of our main sources of food. For the last week the weather has been so wet and miserable that the regular supplies of food and equipment have not been flown up from Collins. Some men would like to leave and are just hanging around the camp waiting for the weather to clear.

After lunch I left my tent in the base camp, which is across the bay from the construction site, to return with the men going back to work. I would have left earlier but there were no boats available — everything has to be ferried back and forth across the bay between the construction site and the base camp, a trip usually delayed by an increasing shortage of boats. Most of the afternoon was spent on the construction site, detailing the composition of work crews, their activities and so on. Most of the twenty or so men on the site were preparing the foundations for the main lodge and four hexagonal-shaped guest cabins. Another crew was in the bush cutting logs (there are already hundreds stacked up along the shoreline) and gathering rocks and sand for the masonry work.

The pace of the work at the construction site is uneven. Some men seem to be confused as to what work was required of them, and there was an obvious lack of decisive, over-all leadership. The site supervisor, who is responsible for these matters, spends much of his time alone preoccupied with the site's engineering problems. Noticed that when certain men would finish their work on a particular task, such as digging a trench, they would sit down for a while and have a cigarette, looking about as if they felt uneasy about not having anything more to do. They would then start wandering around "visiting" others who were working, at which time the inactivity became contagious. In these instances work ground to a halt until the wanderers left, then a flurry of activity as workers tried to catch up. No one has assumed the authority to direct the activities of other workers on the site, as most of the group altered between working and watching.

I then went to spend some time talking with the engineer, thinking that it would be interesting to get his perspective as to what was happening on the site. The engineer was under a tree by the dock, a position overlooking the construction site, where he was working on an intricate scale model of the tourist lodge made from little sticks and pieces of plastic. He smiled and tried to give a cheery picture of the project so far, but he gave up the pretense when I pointed out the obvious difficulties. To paraphrase, his response was as follows: "You can see as well as I can. There is not enough men, there is not enough equipment, there is not enough food, there is not enough good weather... there is not enough of everything. As it is we are getting way behind schedule and my brother's going to be mad as hell. ARDA's never going to go along with this. I think I'm going to have to go to Collins to make sure things get moving again. You know ORG is responsible for hiring the men and moving the equipment up here—they're not doing their job, and it's hurting the project." [The engineer did return to Collins a few days later, but Tom and John McTavish talked him into going back to the site by reassuring him that the resumption of good flying weather would clear up their problems. We discontinued the conversation at that point and I returned to the site to continue my note-taking.]

Part of the problem here is that on this project there is a shortage of experience that could be used as a basis for leadership. In the past, leadership went to the most experienced male in a group, who led by example. But now new skills are needed, since most men have not worked on a construction site before, and few have any direct knowledge of work roles and their supervision in an industrial setting. In contrast to work activities on the lodge site proper, the crew working in the bush cutting logs is better organized. Two ORG foremen travel in close proximity to the shoreline measuring and felling suitable spruce and jack pine. Two other workers follow behind, delimbing and carrying trees to the shore, while three more men debark and otherwise prepare logs for transportation to the construction site. These men spend most of their work day in the bush, which insulates them somewhat from the problems on the construction site. Their jobs in the bush are more clear cut, and they have a more positive perspective on the progress of the project. Men on bush work know what is expected of them, which is something lacking in men on the site.

Another reason for the more satisfactory performance of the bush crew is that in bush-related activities the problem of dominant/submissive work roles is less noticeable than on the site itself. In the bush there is no "boss," in the sense of one person directing the actions of all the other crew members, only more experienced men suggesting appropriate ways by which younger men can more effectively carry out the tasks.

Problems on the construction site, especially supplies of food and a shortage of boats, were not solved as quickly as the engineer had hoped. Some of the supplies were waiting in Armstrong, the end of the road from Thunder Bay, without instructions about whether they should be delivered to Whitewater or Collins. Many men that ORG had hoped to hire from surrounding communities had already found jobs as fire-fighters, tree planters, or tourist guides. This meant fewer men than ever on the construction site because by the late summer there was no ready source of replacement for the men who occasionally left the site. Unemployed white workers were brought in from Thunder Bay, but they met the satisfaction of the engineer even less than Indian workers. Most white workers did not stay long in any event. As one said on parting, "The work's not all that hard, but the black flies up here drive you just about crazy. They're at you all the time, in your coffee, up your nose. I'm sick of the smell of fly dope."

On the first of September, a Sunday, I was awakened by loud shouting in front of my tent. (I stayed at the base camp, occupied by the engineer, two woman cooks, Steve [the bush foreman] and about a dozen other single men. The base camp is across the bay, about a quarter of a mile, from the construction site, and as such a boat is an essential means of transportation.) Steve and the engineer were having an argument over the use of a boat—each man had a grip on either side. A large crowd, the rest of the base camp population, started to gather on the rocks overlooking the make-shift dock. Some were even making themselves comfortable in a sitting position, as if they expected to be there for some time, enjoying some sort of play or public entertainment. The engineer lowered his voice, explaining to Steve that he only wanted to visit Wendel (an elderly white hermit who lives on the other side of Whitewater Lake, about ten miles from the construction site). After all, it was Sunday, not a day of work.

Steve had been harbouring minor grudges against the young engineer for most of the summer, but for the most part he kept them to himself. With the people on the rocks eager to hear more, Steve embraced the opportunity to expose the engineer's shortcomings:

You, the camp boss, want to go on a pleasure trip to the other side of the lake. You will be gone all day, and we will be stuck here because there aren't enough boats. Have you forgotten who brings the fish to camp every day? Well I need a boat now, to go fishing with my brother and [pointing to the rocks] the other men around here. If you go sight-seeing, we'll go hungry—is that what you want? Anyway this boat doesn't belong to ORG, it's Robert's [one of the other ORG foremen] property. Shouldn't you ask him about it first, before you go taking off across the lake as if the boat were yours?

At this point Steve released his grip on the boat, and when he raised his arm to emphasize a point the engineer pushed the craft into the water and sped away. The engineer's decisive move caught Steve in mid-sentence, and he looked a bit embarrassed. The crowd left, regarding the incident a win in neither man's favour.

In these last two months before winter the engineer showed as forceful a personality as he had during the boat-borrowing incident. He became increasingly determined to take charge over the behaviour of the workers on the site, thinking that more control would lead to greater efficiency. As he related:

I think I can get things back on the right track here. The reason for our problem is that there is a leadership vacuum—nobody wants to tell anybody else what to do. It's not much better in Collins. Allen [one of the McTavish brothers, and ORG accountant] is here all the time, but we hardly ever see Tom or John [McTavish]. They don't seem to want to exert too much influence on the men—when they come up here they just stroll around.

The engineer continued to blame ORG for slowdowns on the site because he thought its leaders should have made alternate flying arrangements. But when he became preoccupied with supervising the work crews, he was no longer able to effectively handle the engineering problems (placing sewer lines under tennis courts), and so his performance in both roles declined. By the middle of September the engineer had developed a short temper with the men and, in contrast to his more congenial manner of previous months, spent much of his free time in seclusion.

The Indian workers had difficulty in understanding the engineer's change of attitude. They realized that the pace of work could probably go faster, but they also regarded construction activities as a "learning experience." One cannot learn how to perform the myriad of new skills required, and the appropriate deferential behaviour to outside authorities, in a few weeks. For these reasons Indian workers felt that they should not be held in contempt by the engineer just because they lacked experience and training. They also pointed out that construction activities progressed satisfactorily in those areas where traditional skills could be applied, such as in the bush crew.

Overall, Indian workers felt that the engineer was not justified in asserting authority over "traditionally-oriented" activities since, in their minds, they were the experts. They were willing to grant the engineer authority in those areas of construction of which they themselves had little direct knowledge. Indian workers were also willing to grant him authority for another reason—to avoid the "social costs" of leadership. That is, Ojibwa foremen generally do not wish to emulate white leaders who are viewed as "order-givers" or "pushy." Were an Indian foreman to act in this manner he would probably feel some resentment from fellow workers. According to Collins people, when a person starts ordering other people about they call him *umptigoshe-kauso*, which means "to act like a white man," which in most cases is used as a term of derision.

Besides avoiding the social costs of new work roles, Indian foremen have also found that they can gain some esteem in the eyes of fellow workers when they provoke confrontation with outside authorities if, in their opinion, the authorities have acted beyond the bounds of their particular areas of expertise. The foreman who spent his free time fishing for the camp was on particularly solid ground, politically speaking, by confronting the engineer over the boat borrowing incident. By seizing the appropriate opportunity, the foreman was able to both support the importance of traditional activities and to denigrate the engineer's frivolous pastimes. In effect, the Ojibwa foreman was letting the engineer know that his authority was not necessarily accepted in all areas of camp life, while at the same time enhancing his own position as a leader.

The fact that Indian workers were willing to grant the engineer authority in some areas of camp work, but not in others, is an important observation for this discussion. It suggests that the authority structure which emerged on the construction site was the result of a multiplicity of factors, some stemming from outside influences and others from the local socio-cultural base. Both Indian and outside personnel came to realize that they could not make decisions with impunity or without taking into consideration the costs of interaction with other members of the camp social organization. Ojibwa foremen realized that they must maintain orderly relations with other members of their community after the construction phase of the project is over. They knew that other community members valued their individual autonomy; thus Ojibwa leaders avoid situations where they would be forced to control the behaviour of others overtly. On the other hand, the engineer learned that he would not receive the co-operation of Indian workers on those occasions when they felt resentment towards him. He had to learn to avoid workers' resentment, then, if he was to successfully complete the project and thereby satisfy the desires of his superiors in Toronto.

The situation then was one where both sides were apt to modify their behaviour so as to achieve their own goals. The question raised by this situation is this: If the Ojibwa view the exercise of strong leadership positions as an infringement on one's freedom, then why did they tolerate the engineer's activities? The answer is that from the Ojibwas' perspective the activities of outside bosses are considered necessary in the Ojibwa pursuit of economic viability for their community—they were willing to tolerate a hierarchy of authority relationships in order to facilitate the construction of the tourist lodge. Since leadership by example is a traditional norm, Ojibwa workers are willing to grant authority to outsiders who have expertise in construction work, such as the electricians, stone masons, or plumbers, and who therefore have a claim on leadership by virtue of this expertise.

After the first summer of work was terminated in late September, most of the workers returned to their home communities. Their wives and children had already preceeded them by a month because of the start of the school year. The men looked forward to an autumn of successful moose hunting, content with the fact that most were promised jobs at Whitewater Lake the following spring. Two ORG foremen, whose trap lines border on Whitewater Lake, were hired as caretakers of the tourist lodge property and spent the winter there. Allen McTavish, the bookkeeper, and a third ORG foreman were retained on the payroll to transport supplies by snowmachine from the rail line at Collins to the Whitewater construction site.

Tom and John McTavish spent most of their time that winter talking about how to improve the organization of work at the camp for the following summer. Their first decision was to hire a construction boss from Toronto, an even-tempered, elderly man with decades of experience in the trade. He took pride in teaching construction skills, and by the end of the following summer he was held in high regard by most workers, especially the younger ones. At first they were not sure what to do about the engineer; as John related: "He [the engineer] could be a real problem for us next summer. What if he decides to fight with K. [the new construction boss] all the time . . . challenging his authority. Actually I think he might do all right, if we can convince him not to bother with trying to run the place, and stick to his engineering job." The young engineer agreed to return to work under ORG conditions, and when I talked to him he showed relief at not having to be a "boss" anymore. As events turned out, the engineer got along well with the new construction boss, and, since he concentrated more fully on engineering work, had very few conflicts with the other men as well. For the first time, the engineer seemed happy at what he was doing, now that his role or duties were clarified and ORG leaders were exerting more authority of their own.

ORG leaders also decided to re-organize the work crews to have at least one experienced person in charge of each activity. The bush crews remained much the same as they were the previous summer, although new crews were formed to handle the masonry, carpentry, mechanical, and plumbing work. Collins men filled most supervisory roles, even though more than half of the workers the next summer were from places other than Collins. As the buildings started to emerge above the foundations, it was evident that workers now felt a new sense of accomplishment.

The Ambivalence of Leadership

The McTavish brothers spent a lot of time after the first summer's work thinking about the lessons they had learned, and the problems that still remained. The confusion or feeling of ambivalence expressed by the McTavish brothers was, in my mind, uncharacteristic of their behaviour. They had always appeared confident in dealing with both outsiders and local people, but the situation arising from the Whitewater construction unsettled them. In Collins they were on their own turf, so to speak, a place where they knew how to operate. However, the Whitewater Lake project lacked clear-cut rules. Part of the problem arose from ORG's dependence on skilled outsiders, such as the engineers, who were not directly accountable to ORG since the provincial government paid their wages. Assessments about the quality of this skilled work, however, seemed to fall into a grey area, somewhere between the jurisdictions of the government agency (ARDA) and ORG.

A related problem is that the expectations of the outside workers and local people were often contradictory and fraught with unexpected confusion. For example, it is a common practice among the Ojibwa of northern Ontario when meeting a plane at the dock for the people to line up according to their relative status in the community. In Collins it is almost always one or all of the McTavish brothers who are the first down to the dock. But at the Whitewater site it is usual for the construction supervisor (an outsider) to meet arriving planes. On one occasion it happened that John McTavish was visiting the site and, upon hearing an approaching plane, began to jog down to the dock. When the plane taxied up close both John and the construction boss found themselves uncomfortably situated at the head of the line. The construction boss then backed up a few steps, acceding to John's high status as an ORG official. But what happened when the door of the plane opened was totally unexpected.

Out stepped two smartly dressed men in white hardhats, representatives of a Winnipeg electrical firm which had a $40,000 government contract for work on the lodge. The first one to step out took a look at John and quite casually addressed him as "Boy." No one could believe their ears. After a long pause, John retorted somewhat nervously, "I'm no boy—I'm the boss!" The electrician then tried to slough it off by explaining that this was just his way of talking; no offense intended. The explanation hung in the air like a sooty cloud. The electrical people then ambled down the trail with the construction boss while John stood rooted at the dock, apparently unsure about where he should go.

It was situations like this that made John withdraw into his Collins-based "behind-the-scenes" role, despite the fact that he knew that both the construction boss and the workers commented on the desirability of John making more frequent visits to the site. Such visits bolstered the prestige of the construction boss in the eyes of local workers, and demonstrated that ORG officials really cared about what was going on up there. Problems relating to supervision, jurisdiction, and authority weighed on John's mind well into the winter months. Right after the Christmas holidays I received a letter from John— which at the time surprised me because he almost never writes letters—ostensibly to wish me season's greetings. But within a few lines he began to express his concerns about the Whitewater project, especially in relation to the outsider's supervisory activities on the construction site. Here, then, in John's words are some of his thoughts during early January (1975):

The Whitewater Wilderness Lodge Project has ground to a halt as of Oct. 30th but will try to do some winter building starting this week. Seems to be some doubt as to whether a log can be pealed in the dead of winter we shall see soon. I myself have never tried to do this but sure hope logs are peelable then. We have been given a one month trial from the boys BOYS ah hem I mean gentlemen from Toronto. ARDA seems to go along with the idea. Design 44 [the Toronto-based engineering firm discussed in the preceding section] is another matter. If it is possible and we can build without a rep from 44 it opens up possibilities. I don't think we could do entirely without some sort of engineer sometimes but for the most part maybe someone could come in every ten days or so for a few days. T. [the young engineering student, employed by his elder brother and director of Design 44] was getting $80.00 a day for his part last summer. At least that is what 44 was charging for his services. What does an anthropologist get?

We got a LIP grant to finish our experimental house and maintain our winter trail to Whitewater. We are spreading too thin. Soon it will all crumble down on our heads.

The letter illustrates John's oft-repeated concerns about how to effectively deal with outside experts upon whom one is dependent, but who are not controlled by or accountable to the local population. The reference to "boys BOYS ah hem I mean gentlemen" is an obvious reference to the incident on the Whitewater Lodge dock, which months later still troubled John, and to the general atmosphere of condescension with which the McTavish brothers have to cope in their dealings with the outside world. John also expresses the sentiment that ORG needs the skills of outsiders, but not those who spend a great deal of their time assuming the posture of a boss. John further feels that the engineering student is overpaid for his services, but that there is nothing ORG can do about it because Design 44 sends its bill to ARDA rather than to ORG. The letter ends on a sanguine note, probably because ARDA had not as yet agreed to provide the funds required to complete the construction of the lodge. Thus, John and his brothers were continually forced to make concrete plans for activities and projects with little assurance that they would actually take place. It was this burden of uncertainty concerning the in-flow of funds, coupled with numerous factors over which ORG was not allowed to exercise control, which led, in John's case, to a sense of impending doom.

By early spring ARDA eventually allocated funds for the summer's construction work, which helped to alleviate ORG anxieties. But despite assurances that work on the lodge would continue for at least the next five or six months, John's ambivalent feelings towards his role on the construction site became even more pronounced than they were the previous summer. John's "visits" to Whitewater became even less frequent than before, and when he did arrive I found it peculiar that he was equipped with a camera and fishing rod (I have never seen John fishing). He seemed to be adopting the role of a tourist, someone with only a passing interest in the construction activities. It was almost as if his feelings of ambivalence forced him to adopt a new role, one which would reduce the possibilities of any overt conflict between himself and the on-site supervisors.

This did not mean that John was not interested in the lodge project; in fact, despite his casual appearance, the exact opposite was the case. His main concern was to not appear to be checking up on the site supervision or to use his position on the ORG executive to "Lord it over" the engineer and construction boss. To illustrate the peculiarities of this developing situation, on one occasion I went down to greet John at the Whitewater dock. I suggested that we make a tour of the site together so that I could get his response concerning the recent changes.

I was surprised that he did not want any part of such a tour and instead suggested that we walk over to the small store that his brother Allen operated. Once inside the store he took up a position next to the wall and began peering through the cracks between the logs. John spent the afternoon in that position, squinting through binoculars, occasionally commenting on this or that aspect of the construction work. As time went on he became increasingly aggravated over what he perceived to be a lackadaisical flow in the construction work. By the end of the afternoon he began to articulate the source of his frustration; to paraphrase him:

This whole situation is getting ridiculous, don't you think? A herd of snails could get the work done faster. What are we supposed to do anyway? If I go out there and tell T [the student engineer] or M. [the construction foreman] to smarten up and get their act together they'll just get mad and quit or something. Then they'll probably go and tell ARDA that I'm a meddler and the cause of the work slowdowns. They did that before and ARDA almost didn't give us any more money. What are we supposed to do anyway? When things go wrong ORG gets the blame, and when things go alright ARDA praises the engineer. Look out there [pointing to one of the larger cracks], the men are caught in the middle—they don't know who's running the show. And come to think of it, I can't say that I know any more either.

John's remark that the men on the construction site were caught in the middle of a jurisdictional dispute was an accurate assessment of the situation because many of the men expressed this as a problem also, and on one occasion they tried to do something about improving the work situation. Early on in the second summer of work a dispute developed between the young engineer and the construction foreman. The foreman threatened to resign and temporarily left the site. This situation was viewed as a serious matter by the workers and they proceeded to draft a petition in support of the foreman who, in contrast to the engineer, was well liked by the men. This action was applauded by the McTavish brothers because for some time they had been trying to think of ways to restrict the influence of the young engineer. This was just the sort of situation that they had hoped for because they now had some clear evidence that the activities of the engineer threatened to undermine the project as a whole. This situation then became the focal point of a subsequent meeting with ARDA and Design 44 officials who were persuaded to accept ORG recommendations that the engineer's influence had to be curtailed for the good of the project. Eventually a proclamation was posted at the Whitewater camp clearly indicating that the foreman had ultimate authority over the engineer.

The petition was a hot topic of conversation around the camp for several weeks. The men as a whole felt that they had done the right thing, and I began to sense a new feeling of involvement on the workers' part, a feeling that what they had to say mattered. This was also the sort of situation for which the McTavish brothers had been waiting: it was rare that Design 44 and ARDA had to agree with an ORG assessment of the situation. However, there was an added reason why the McTavish brothers were pleased—the construction foreman realized that it was to ORG that he owed the reinstatement of his job with an increased level of authority. The lines of authority began to take a new form, such that the foreman was now more directly accountable to ORG, and ARDA's man on the job (the engineer) suffered a diminuation of influence.

Restructuring Lines of Authority

Prior to the advent of ORG, authority and power relationships in the Collins community were diffuse and unco-ordinated. The fur trader, the McTavish brothers' father, was able to exert influence through his dual role as fur broker and store operator. However, this influence could only be exercised when the people were actually camping on Collins Lake, usually only for the summer months. Missionaries have always made only infrequent visits to the community and up until recent times there were a number of incidents where ministers were openly ridiculed (some of which are documented by a minister himself [Baldwin, 1957]). The CNR as the village's only full-time employer was certainly in a position of influence, but only to the extent that men were on the job and working for the company. However, this influence has diminished somewhat as labour requirements lessened in conjunction with the fact that few men in the settlement stayed on the job for more than a couple of years. The only source of perdurable influences emanated from men in their role as household and family heads. This influence though could only be exercised among their close kin on the trapline or in the village. All in all, Collins was one of those small backwoods communities where each family ran their own affairs in relative isolation from external influence.

The rise of ORG heralded a new era by transforming existing sources of influence into a larger sphere of organization. Formerly autonomous household heads were integrated into a larger structure which, for the time being at least, served to transcend the dividing lines of kin group, band affiliation, or Indian status. ORG also effectively linked the local community to external governmental agencies as it tapped the financial and experiential resources of the larger society. ORG leaders tried to forge a mediating role in this transfer of resources, and sought to parley this role into a cross-cutting source of local influence. But, as we have seen so far, playing the intermediary role in order to consolidate local power can lead to a situation where the occupier of this role can be caught in the middle like a fly in a web of ambivalence and indecision.

Of the ORG leaders, John McTavish was one of the first to recognize the pitfalls of the middle position. He correctly surmised the situation as one where financial assistance from government would be extended hand-in-hand with outside control agents. Initially the control agents, in the form of representatives from ARDA and Design 44, were ostensibly employed as facilitators of the local project. But as time went on it became evident, to John at least, that these agents were building the base of influence in local affairs to the point where the continued integrity of ORG was severely threatened. This was accomplished by attempts to make ORG look as if it were incompetent to run local projects, both in the eyes of ARDA and ORG workers. As John saw it, this was a crisis of confidence. If it were allowed to continue, ORG would eventually be shunted entirely away from a position where it played any role at all in the important decisions effecting Collins people. ORG would have become a somnambulant shell, routinely paying wages and sending back taxes, incapable of making decisions which in any way compromised interests outside the village. ORG would have been stripped of the very genius and organizational drive which had led to such important gains in the first place. In one of my many conversations with John he summed up the situation this way:

I don't understand what all the fuss is about. If all the government wanted to do was build a tourist lodge why didn't they just hire a construction company to come and do it for us. Sure, it would have been built almost overnight, but it would not have been what we wanted and we wouldn't have had a clue about how to operate it. I guess then they would have hired the managers and workers to run it. Where do the Collins people come into this scheme of things? I thought that the government gave us this money so that we could learn how to do things for ourselves—sort of like an on-the-job training program. There have been mistakes and cost overruns, that's true, but we've learned a lot so far; anyway the cost hasn't been excessive—ARDA spends that much to build a parking lot for one of its shopping plazas. We've all been pretty naive up until now, but let me tell you that if we don't start doing something right now the whole thing—the lodge, ORG, everything—will go right down the tube.

This, then, was the reasoning behind a more activist and interventionist posture by the ORG executive. Overall, it sought to more effectively entrench ORG in an intercalary position between the financial backers (ARDA) on the outside and the Design 44 representatives stationed at Whitewater Lake. This task was in part accomplished by restricting the influence of the young engineer and bolstering the position of the construction foreman. Thus, one developing line of authority (ARDA → site engineer → workers) was restructured so as to assume a new form (ARDA → ORG → construction foreman → workers), thereby reinstating ORG as a principle actor in the White-water project.

The restructuring of authority relationships began at the management level (i.e., engineer and construction foreman) but ORG also thought that it would be in their interest to then focus on a reorganization of the worker population at Whitewater Lake. One of the main reasons why this was considered necessary, aside from a desire to make workers more productive, was that considerably more workers were required than initially anticipated. This resulted in the hiring of many men from outside the Collins community, men who owed no particular allegiance to ORG and who could be manipulated by the engineer. Since there were times when Collins people formed a minority of the worker population at Whitewater, it was considered necessary by ORG to place their own people, or outsiders loyal to ORG, in positions of authority.

To give an example, the workers were organized into a number of crews that had specific tasks to perform. A bush crew consisting of about ten men was responsible for cutting logs and transporting them to the site. A smaller crew of five men worked on the construction of the main lodge, while another crew of about the same size was busy building the tourist cabins. A crew of eight older men spent most of their time peeling logs (of which over 30,000 were required to build the facilities). On all four of these crews Collins men were made crew foremen, men who had all worked for ORG on various other projects in the preceding years. For the most part, workers in these crews were non-Collins men. There were also a number of smaller crews involved in more specialized activities, such as masonry and electrical and plumbing work. In these latter cases outsiders, mainly Eurocanadians from Thunder Bay and Toronto, were the foremen but the crews consisted of Collins men. Thus, even though Collins men formed a minority in the work force population their authority overall was increased by elevations to the position of crew foremen, while in smaller, more specialized crews Collins men could "keep and eye on" their Eurocanadian foremen. This restructuring of authority relations emanating from outside served to once again place ORG as the paramount authority in the Whitewater construction project.

Consolidating the Work Force

A Whitewater work force in which Collins people were in a minority was a situation not originally anticipated by ORG, and was a source of mounting concern by its executive. The McTavish brothers were especially concerned that this situation would lead to a loss of control and influence on the part of ORG. Initially the ORG plan called for the construction work to be carried on entirely by Collins workers, even if more time than usual would be required. ORG had conceived of the project as one for Collins people , in that most of the funding allocated for labour costs should go into the pockets of Collins workers. ARDA, mainly on the prompting of the site engineer, insisted that a work schedule had to be maintained, and this could only be accomplished with a full complement of workers. From the ORG perspective this meant that Collins people could no longer be the main beneficiaries in either monetary or experiential terms. It was also felt that hiring numerous outsiders would serve to diminish the authority of ORG among the outsiders who might be led to believe that it was ARDA and Design 44, and not ORG, who were building the tourist lodge. However, a high turnover of men during the first summer of work made ORG's initial plan untenable and its executive began to augment the work force with men from neighbouring communities. The idea was that this hiring should be made selective so that men would be hired from communities where the people knew of ORG activities. It was also felt that it should be ORG that did the actual hiring so that workers would appear to owe their jobs to ORG, rather than to ARDA or Design 44.

A comparison of the Whitewater Lake work force during the first two summers of work helps to illustrate some of the problems faced by ORG on the construction project. At the beginning of the first summer's work there were slightly over fifteen people working on the site and these were all from Collins. Due to complaints from the site engineer, ARDA began to put pressure on ORG to increase the work force. In August (1974) I conducted a census of the Whitewater camp population which revealed the following:

Total camp population	72
Workers' dependents	39
Number of workers	33
From: Collins	19
Mud River	11
Armstrong	3

In addition, there were two Collins men on Whitewater Lake (and their families) working as fishing guides for an Armstrong tourist operator. On nearby Shapuskwia Lake an additional two Collins men were also working as guides out of their fishing camp. All four of these men subsequently worked for ORG the following summer, three of them as ORG foremen.

Interviews were then conducted with John and Tom McTavish about their decisions concerning additions to the Collins work force at Whitewater. Why, I asked, were additional workers hired mainly from Mud River (a small community of about a hundred people on the CNR line forty miles east of Collins)? The reasoning was the same in both interviews. They both related that after their father had quit his job as the HBC post manager at Fort Hope in the mid-1940s he took his family to Mud River where he had bought a store and tourist outfitter's operation. Mud River people, according to the McTavish brothers, are good workers, know about the tourist business, and are not trouble-makers. The McTavish brothers still remember many of these people as childhood friends and playmates. The three Armstrong men are also familiar to the McTavish brothers—the father of one of these had once operated the store in Collins and another is the chief of the widely dispersed White Sand Band. I concluded from these interviews that if ORG had to hire workers from outside the Collins work force, a move that the McTavish brothers did not entirely agree with, then these men should come from a place such as Mud River where the McTavish brothers still "had connections" through their father's role as patron and employer. I also sensed that Mud River people are regarded by the McTavish brothers as something like a distant family. At one point Tom McTavish remarked, "Mud River people are good workers, it's just that nobody has ever given them a chance," which I took as an apparent reference to Tom's feeling that Collins people also had not been "given a chance" in the past. In this context "given a chance" refers to the relatively high level of unemployment in both Collins and Mud River prior to the Whitewater project.

In sum, by the end of the first summer of work the Collins work force at the Whitewater site was augmented by men from neighbouring communities who were familiar with ORG and its operations, and among whom the McTavish brothers felt they were able to exercise some influence, mainly through their own and their father's previous contacts with the Mud River people. Augmenting the work force at Whitewater was therefore regarded as a non-threatening situation for ORG because Collins people still formed a numerical majority and workers from outside could be easily placed under ORG's network of local influence.

The situation the following summer was considerably different. ARDA, through the urging of the site engineer, expressed a desire to expand the Whitewater work force beyond what it had been the previous summer. This led to the hiring of many men who knew little or nothing about Collins and ORG. From the ORG perspective this meant a considerable dilution of its network of influence and a gravitation of many new workers into the engineer's sphere of influence. A situation, then, where Collins workers were in a minority position and where ORG's influence was diminishing was regarded by the McTavish brothers as a matter of serious concern.

A census conducted at the end of the second summer of work (September 1975) revealed the following composition of the Whitewater work force:

Number of workers	51
From: Collins	18
Fort Hope	10
Armstrong	8
Mud River	7
Gull Bay	3
outside region	5

Overall, the Collins and Mud River worker population remained much the same as the previous summer. Armstrong workers more than doubled in number (from 3 to 8), and 5 workers from outside the region found their way to Whitewater Lake.

The biggest change from the previous year was the addition of the Fort Hope men and their families to the camp population. The first of these to arrive were two middle-aged men, one of whom was a former resident of Collins, who had taken their canoes down from Fort Hope in order to find work. Shortly after, Tom McTavish flew up to Fort Hope and hired a dozen additional workers. Fort Hope workers are regarded in a similar light by the McTavish brothers as the Mud River people. The McTavish brothers were born in Fort Hope themselves and, as already mentioned, their father was the HBC post manager there for ten years. In addition, their mother was also born and raised there and was a member of the local Fort Hope elite. Tom also expressed the opinion that Fort Hope men were diligent workers who, because of Fort Hope's remote location, were familiar with life in the bush. In all, the McTavish brothers were anxious to recruit Fort Hope people because of their close ties to Collins and their traditional bush expertise. It also meant that Fort Hope people, like those from Mud River, could be more easily placed in ORG's "sphere of influence" than those unfamiliar with ORG and its operations.

The second summer's work therefore differed from the first in that Collins workers formed a minority of the worker population at the camp. However, the McTavish brothers attempted to counter-balance a possible lessening of their influence by the active recruitment of men who could be integrated into ORG's system of control. The hiring of men from Armstrong (considered by the McTavish brothers as potentially hostile towards the Whitewater project) was a different matter. In an interesting move to obviate potential problems from this group, the McTavish brothers picked one of the most influential Armstrong men, someone who could be counted on to support ORG, and promoted him to the position of crew foreman.

Work Force Turnover

ORG's attempt to recruit a large loyal work force from both inside and outside the Collins community was an ongoing problem upon which the McTavish brothers expended much effort. As such, it was essentially a matter of recruitment, whereas the maintenance of the existing work force was a slightly different but related concern. Early in the second summer of work I was especially interested in collecting data on the length of time individual workers stayed on the job in order to assess the rate of worker turnover. One of ORG's problems was not so much in hiring a certain number of workers, but in hiring workers at a rate which compensated for those leaving the work site. I also considered it useful to compare the community of origin of those workers who stayed for long periods of time with that of those who stayed for only a short while. This material, I figured, would yield a basis for judging the accuracy of the McTavish brother's assessment about which workers could be counted on and which could not (if "counted on" were interpreted in terms of length of stay on the job).

In order to compile this material a record was kept for an 11.5-week period (from April 25 to July 13, 1975) early in the second summer of work. Over this period a total of 58 workers were hired, of which 44 workers were still on the job at the end of the period, yielding a turnover rate of 24 percent. In other words, if this pattern also held for the last half of the summer, the number of turnovers would be equivalent to over half of the total work force. Put another way, for every two workers hired an additional one would have to be employed in order to replace the one who would eventually leave. Thus ORG was faced with the prospect of not just hiring a work force of a certain size, but of hiring half as many workers again in order to replace those who would quit in the meantime. Another approach is to calculate the average length of stay per worker, which for the 11.5 week period amounted to 5.8 weeks. Thus, on the average each worker stayed on the job for roughly one-half of the work period. The numerical breakdown for length of employment for Whitewater construction workers is as follows:

under 2 weeks	5
2 to 4 weeks	15
5 to 7 weeks	14
8 to 10 weeks	17
over 10 weeks	7

The next step in the analysis is to examine in more detail the community of origin for those workers in the "under 2 weeks" category, as well as for those in the "over 10 weeks" category. The purpose is to find out if community of origin could be used as a predictor of which workers could be expected to leave early and which would stay on to the end of the summer. In addition, a community-of-origin analysis was conducted on all workers who left before the end of the 11.5 week period.

For workers remaining on the job for less than two weeks, two came from Mud River, two from Collins, and one from Fort Hope. Actually the two Collins men might be excluded from this category as one rehired a short time later, and the other was Joe Tobano, the CNR foreman, who was working at Whitewater on his vacation. If we now examine the fourteen men leaving before the end of the period under consideration, seven are from Mud River, two each from Collins, Fort Hope, and outside the region, and one from Gull Bay. For workers who stayed beyond ten weeks, five are from Collins, and one each from Armstrong and Mud River.

What do these figures tell us about the Whitewater work force? For one thing, they tell us that the confidence placed in the Mud River workers by the McTavish brothers is probably unwarranted as these workers seem to be among the first to leave. It is quite possible, however, that many of these men had made prior commitments to work for tourist operators in the Mud River area. Tourists do not usually begin arriving until the latter part of June and most of them leave by the early part of August, at which time Mud River workers may rehire at Whitewater Lake. The figures also tell us, not surprisingly perhaps, that Collins workers are among the most dependable, since most workers in the "over 10 week" category are from this community. Assessments about Fort Hope workers' "loyalty" are more difficult to gauge because most of them fall into the middle range of weeks worked. It should be noted, however, that most Fort Hope men were still working at the end of this period. Most seem to hire on about a month after the start-up date, probably a result of early spring commitments back home, such as the maintenance of fish camps during the spawning season.

The final step in the analysis determines which workers enumerated in the spring census were still working when the September count was made. This yields a sort of "worker attrition index," or what ORG leaders might consider somewhat of a "loyalty index." As indicated in Table 17, of the 58 workers employed at the Whitewater construction site in the spring (1975) only 25 of these were still employed in the fall. Thus, there was an overall attrition rate of the work force of 57 percent or, put another way, more workers left their jobs than stayed for the entire summer period. In terms of community of origin, Collins workers were the most likely to stay for the whole summer while those from Fort Hope and outside the area were the least likely to remain. In fact, there is a direct correspondence in this chart between attrition rate and distance of the home community from the Whitewater site. After Collins, Armstrong is closest, followed by Mud River, Gull Bay and so on. As a general rule then, the farther away the worker's community of origin is from the construction site, the greater will be the chance that the worker will leave before the end of the summer work period.

TABLE 17

Work Force Attrition Rate, Whitewater Lake, 1975

Workers' community of origin	On job (Spring)	Still on job (Fall)	Attrition rate (%)
Collins	17	13	24
Armstrong	10	5	50
Mud River	15	6	60
Gull Bay	7	1	86
Fort Hope	4	0	100
Outside area	5	0	100
Totals	58	25	(Avg.) 57

The significance of these calculations is that, in terms of ORG leaders' perceptions of worker "loyalty," these perceptions would appear to be an unreliable predictor of the length of time workers can be expected to stay on the job. A far more reliable predictor would be in terms of the distance that a worker must travel to the construction site, with those travelling the shortest distance staying the longest, and those travelling the farthest staying the shortest period of time. Given the high turnover rate at the Whitewater construction site, ORG would be well advised to hire as many workers as possible from Armstrong, regardless of what they might think of the people from that community. By contrast, workers from Mud River and Fort Hope, who are held in high regard by the McTavish brothers, have an overall attrition rate of near 70 percent, which makes workers from these communities not very reliable at all.

Discussion

This case study of the Whitewater project illustrates the many difficulties faced by the leaders of small northern communities who are attempting to initiate local economic development. We are often led to believe that people in such communities have high unemployment and a low standard of living because they lack the initiative to help themselves. The picture is one of a passive northern settlement whose members wait for the government to come in and solve their problems. When government-sponsored projects fail it is almost always the local residents who are seen, in the eyes of government representatives, to be responsible for the difficulties.

The northern native population is commonly portrayed as somewhat backward, mired in past traditions, and generally inept at dealing with the changing modern world. One tires of reading the "executive summaries" of government reports where the significant barriers to change in the North concentrate on certain loosely-defined psychological or social factors that are perceived to exist among native people, such as problems relating to punctuality or community responsibilities restricting greater participation in the wage economy. In such reports there is hardly ever an effort made to examine the advantages of maintaining economic diversity, such as combining subsistence production with commercial activity—most of the effort seeks merely to change local attitudes or behaviour in order to minimize disruptions in official planning.

Those who have spent time living in a northern native settlement are apt to feel uneasy about the government's "modernist" perspective on community development. Experience has taught that what the outsiders call barriers or obstructions to development are better understood not in the context of national economic expansion, but in the context of locally perceived opportunities and restrictions. The modernist approach is also apt to lead research away from important areas of concern, such as the benefits to be derived by using local resources or the contribution of traditional economic activity to the viability of northern community life. If anything, what has often been overlooked by the larger society has been the initiatives that native peoples themselves are taking to overcome their problems. Additionally, we are also led to overlook situations where it has been the government representative, through lack of knowledge or sensitivity to local concerns, who acts as the barrier or impediment to the successful completion of a project. The academic literature, too, has largely ignored or failed to document local initiative in northern areas, or to analyse these efforts in the wider sphere of political and economic change. In my mind there are lessons in such cases as the Collins project for governmental people as well as the social scientist.

One of these lessons is the formidable task facing leaders, even in small communities such as Collins, of embarking on a long-term program of local development by people trained for the most part as storekeepers, trappers, and tourist guides. Take for example a limited aspect of a project such as hiring workers. It is not simply a matter of hiring the best from among a large pool of unemployed people, but of trying to meet the often conflicting needs of a population with a diversity of income sources. How could a local leader deny people the time to hunt or fish when he realizes that more economic benefit ("income") is derivable from these short-term activities than from a more steady but lower paying job that the leader might make available?

The best solution is to make wage employment available when people need it most, which for many northern residents occurs during slack periods in the game-subsistence cycle. Another possibility is for some people to hunt and fish while others are engaged in wage work, and then to alternate the people engaged in these occupations over different periods of time. In Collins both of these approaches have been used to keep up a sizeable work force on government-sponsored projects, while simultaneously deriving benefit from an efficient use of local resources.

This strategy, however, while eminently reasonable from a local perspective, has led to no end of conflict with government representatives who want a project completed as quickly as possible. For the most part this means that every unemployed person should be available to work on the government-funded project, and if there are not sufficient workers available from the local community, then the remainder must be hired from other settlements. Collins leaders were willing to do this, even if they did not agree with the approach, rather than jeopardize the project. Since the government agency has the ability to withdraw further funding if Collins leaders did not comply with its directives, few options remain open for such leaders. But perhaps the biggest area of concern is that, while Collins leaders knew something about the reliability of workers from their home community, they had virtually no first-hand experience with workers from other settlements in the area.

The leaders also knew full well that they would only be able to hire those people not successful at finding work at home, which means that prospects for these workers would not be very high. As events turned out, at the Whitewater construction site over half of the workers from these neighbouring communities hired in the spring quit before the end of the season. All in all, there were probably just not enough good

men available in the surrounding communities to continue construction of the lodge according to the pace of the government's work
schedule. Of course the big problem from the perspective of Collins
leaders was that good jobs were being given away to unappreciative
outsiders. This had the effect of reducing benefits for Collins people
themselves, which in their eyes was the only reason for starting the
project in the first place. ARDA wanted to build a tourist lodge as
efficiently and quickly as possible. The goal of the community leaders
was to develop the local economy and work force. From the perspective of Collins people these two goals were potentially compatible, but
really quite different in scope.

Admittedly, the task of government is not at all an easy one. Its
representatives have to deal with all kinds of unknown quantities—
the native people in the area, their skills, knowledge, and probable
chances of completing a complex and expensive project. Government
people involved in the Collins case commonly expressed the idea that
employing people was their objective, and if anything else came of it
then so much the better. This clearly implied that they did not expect
the project to succeed, although they did not say so in as many words.

While both Collins and government people sometimes acted as if
they had forgotten it, "success" for both groups depended a great deal
on their mutual co-operation. Although the situation is not one of
inflexibility on either side, the government does have the funding
which makes the Collins project possible in the first place. In light of
the listing of government cash inputs from 1971-1975 (Table 16), it
does not seem probable that ORG would have flourished without this
monetary support. Understandably, ORG would succeed only so long
as its leaders had the necessary monetary rewards to provide to their
supporters.

A second lesson of the Whitewater project concerns the distribution of power, control, and authority. The power of government representatives derives mainly from their role as financiers, but they also
typically occupy an additional role as planners. This creates a situation
where government and local inputs are largely asymmetric—a situation where the dependency of native people on government is apt to be
increased, rather than lessened, over time. Since the ostensible purpose of government aid is to help native people take better care of
themselves, then it is reasonable that more attention be given to promoting or encouraging the development of local-level leadership
skills. A step in this direction could be made by allowing local leaders
more input into some of the more important decisions that have to be
made, such as how long it will take to complete a project or how many
people will be employed.

In the short term this suggestion could lead to slightly increased costs and a more lengthy construction schedule. But in the long run these costs would be counterbalanced by a more skilled and confident work and leadership organization in the local community. We are prone to forget that members of the local community are not professional planners and craftspeople, and it takes time to develop these skills. By simply hiring outsiders to do the planning and skilled work on the rationale that it is less costly to do so is not going to make the local people any more efficient at conducting their own affairs.

There is something of a self-fulfilling prophecy in all of this—the native population is denied access to and participation in the institutions of power and decision making because they are thought to be not very competent in these areas. In turn, lacking an opportunity to participate in such affairs means that the skills necessary to operate in these areas are not developed, all of which provides the justification for continued agency dominance of local developmental schemes. Surely the adversarial stance that developed between ORG and ARDA, especially between the McTavish brothers and the engineers, only served to sap the energies of both parties. If anything constructive was accomplished by this ongoing antagonism it was a realization on the part of the McTavish brothers in their role as ORG leaders that the power to change things only accrues to those with the will to become actively involved, and that a persistent and skillful promotion of one's interests and wishes does have a payoff.

Conclusion

Collins's centralized leadership structure, mainly involving the trader's three sons and their close associates, played an important role in initiating economic change in the community. It brought new money into the local economy and provided new sources of employment. It established new community goals—such as self-employment through a locally-based tourist enterprise—and the organizational framework for achieving them.

A large part of this success can be attributed to the qualities and capabilities of the trader's sons. They have the skills and experience to satisfy external funding agencies, and have emerged as Collins's main contact point with the outside world. Their ability to operate in the outside world is something other people in Collins have difficulty doing, and for this reason one could consider the brothers as quasi-outsiders. In this characteristic they resemble Dunning's (1959b) "marginal men"; the traders and missionaries who act as local patrons but who remain separate from others in the community. But the three brothers are "marginal men" only to the extent that they have unusual capabilities. Ethnically they are regarded by local people as *anishenabek*, or Indian people, for reasons discussed earlier—their maternal kinship links provide them with blood relatives in the Indian population and they were born and have spent most of their lives in an Indian community. One of the brothers has married into the Collins community, while the other two have local girlfriends. As such, the brothers are more socially integrated into the local community than is the case with any of the "marginal men" described in the literature.

Does this mean that the right personality characteristics would have ensured successful leadership in Collins? Not altogether, because there were other important factors involved. The abilities of Collins leaders were useful mainly in the context of government agencies willing to provide substantial financial backing for local projects, such as those that existed in Canada through the late sixties and early seventies. Without government backing there would have been no new jobs and few reasons for forming ORG in the first place. But Collins had all the "right" characteristics for attracting outside help—high unemployment, cramped living conditions, few local services, and so on. Collins is therefore a case where local abilities and initiative were appropriately matched with governmental aims and objectives. Collins leaders were able to successfully exploit a favourable external environment and, in turn, to direct these abilities towards the achievement of local political and economic ends.

A main reason then for the success of the Collins leadership, in particular the McTavish brothers with their urban contacts, is the use of governmental resources such as DREE and ARDA and the outside political and economic world in general as resources. The McTavish brothers are sufficiently native to secure local support, yet Euro-canadian enough to move successfully in the larger sphere in which their community is encapsulated. But while ORG could only have succeeded because its leaders had rewards to provide to supporters, mobilization of the people also involved considerable skill and leadership. Consolidating an efficient work force at the Whitewater construction site was a constant source of concern, as was the need to continually replenish a work force characterized by a high turnover rate. The authority structure on the construction site was another problem area requiring additional attention on ORG's part. Overall, the supervision of construction work exposed the ambivalent nature of a local leadership not specifically equipped with modern construction skills, but nonetheless desirous of maintaining a certain degree of control and influence over the construction process as a whole.

CHAPTER SIX

Conclusion

Emergent Leadership and Exchange

In this study of the Ogoki River Guides enterprise and the conditions which facilitated its development I have opted for an approach to emergent leadership that uses an "exchange" perspective. The nature of this paradigm and some of the problems associated with its application were discussed in the introductory chapter. It would now be useful to focus on some of the findings of this study in light of the perspective taken on emergent leadership, and thereby to come to some conclusions about the usefulness of this approach as a guide to ethnographic field research.

A main problem concerns the situational, individualistic approach to exchange typified by the work of Peter Blau in sociology and Fredrik Barth in anthropology. Both of these authors have explicitly recognized the importance of individual action in the analysis of social change. In particular, Barth's "generative" model of human behaviour is designed to emphasize the role of individuals in determining the overt form of a particular society. His model is aimed at showing how individuals exercising choice are responsible for creating social organization. Patterned regularities in social behaviour are produced by a convergence of different factors which are seen to influence the choices people make. The issue here concerns the accuracy of explaining the forms of social life as the result of factors governing individual action. As David Easton makes clear, "Exchange theory runs into difficulty if it seeks to demonstrate either the way in which political structures arise and change, or the constraints these structures place on behavior, or the consequences they have for the operation of political systems. Fundamentally the weakness of exchange theory derives from its implicit attempt to substitute psychological explanation of individual behavior for social understanding" (Easton 1972: 137).

Does the exchange perspective then help us to understand the emergence of leadership in Collins? The answer is "Yes, but only

135

partly." If we take a broad or macro view of the Collins situation we find the following general characteristics: a small, relatively isolated native community with a high level of unemployment; government agencies willing to provide funding for local projects which promise to increase employment, providing certain procedures and provisions are followed; and finally, a few individuals from the community willing to serve in a leadership capacity. These leaders have the necessary skills and experience to channel new resources from the larger society to the local population. In this context, how important a factor is individual decision making in changing the Collins situation? There are reasons for thinking that this is a factor of only secondary importance. The main one is that the government aid agencies exercise considerable control, which leaves few options for the local leader. It is the local group that must hope for acceptance by the government agency. In addition, the agency controls the amount of financial assistance, the timetable for the disbursement of the funds, and the form of repayment. Local leaders have an opportunity to influence this arrangement only to a limited degree, and usually through indirect means, such as the use of the news media or members of the legislature willing to act as an advocate on their behalf.

One conclusion then is that a key factor in influencing the economic condition in northern communities involves the initiation of the funding process. Government and local inputs are asymmetric because the initiative for many northern projects, their conception and planning, come from the outside. For native people, the aid agency is not merely a banker who underwrites local schemes; the government agents typically propose them as well. Thus government power derives from its dual role as planner and initiator, as well as that of financier.

The influence of ORG leaders mainly involves the organization of local activity, such as deciding which workers will be hired, and maintaining the supply of goods and equipment to the Whitewater construction site. Thus, when attempting to explain the emergence of leadership in Collins we must focus on the relationship between choices and constraint, especially within the institutional and environmental context in which the choices are made. As far as the Collins case is concerned the decisions that leaders make are best understood in the asymmetric context of local-governmental interaction and exchange.

In the "generative" approach to exchange there is a tendency to assume that each individual is able to pursue their interests as if ideal-type market conditions prevailed. The actor-oriented perspective of exchange theory also tends to view human action as relatively unrestrained by its social systems, relationships, and settings. This study of Collins illustrates that political and economic decisions cannot be adequately understood without a corresponding analysis of the decision maker's assets, access to new resources, and the organizational context in which his or her decisions are made. We must take into account the decisions made by other people, as well as the tendency of people to change or modify their own decisions in the face of the decisions made by more powerful people. In this context not all interests and choices contribute equally to the emergence of social arrangements.

A lesson here is that social relationships cannot be solely understood in terms of people's aims and interests. The reason for this is that the structure and organization of social activity is rarely the result of conscious design. If it were, then we would all have a better chance of living in the utopian settings human beings so frequently desire. In sum, for contemporary exchange theory to rely for its validation on micro-group processes and interaction, then the relationship between these processes and the wider social and environmental systems in which exchange takes place should be made an explicit area of concern. The rationale for this is that our ability to gain knowledge about exchange systems is inhibited by the fact that these wider systems tend to govern, or at least direct, small-group interaction, its content, and the conditions under which it exists.

The conclusions of this study of emergent leadership in terms of the exchange theory approach in anthropology can therefore be summed up as follows:

(1) *Exchange behaviour is a multi-faceted phenomenon.* One can be expected to find various economic, political, social, cultural, and environmental components of exchange. Given particular circumstances, some components will be more significant than others, but in each case exchange situations are "generated" by a combination of factors. These factors act upon one another through time, thus yielding an historical perspective to exchange.

In the Collins case the kinds of exchange that took place in this community are only understandable, as has been argued throughout the book, in terms of a multiplicity of factors. The social organization of the village is divided in various ways, mainly by band membership, which serves to promote exchange within certain groups, but to curtail interaction across group boundaries. However, contemporary marriage patterns, in combination with ORG leaders' attempts to widely distribute incoming resources, have acted as countervailing forces in the possible narrowing of intergroup interaction. The economic dimension of exchange in Collins is also an important consideration.

Resources originating both within and outside the community are distributed in various ways producing a particular pattern to the labour force, worker mobility, consumption characteristics, and so on. The political factors of exchange result largely from the way resources are distributed. Local leaders negotiate with government officials producing patterns of influence. Leaders and followers in Collins are united in a common organization which has its own forms of dependency relations, political strategies, and elite group characteristics. As this description of the Collins case illustrates, exchange is likely to have significant material and social aspects which must be studied together if accurate assessments of particular cases are to be made.

(2) *Exchange behaviour is a social affair.* This point is a corollary of the above discussion, but is worth mentioning in its own right given some of the contemporary perspectives on exchange theory in anthropology. This book in part is a critique of the individualistic, actor-oriented approach to exchange behaviour that is characteristic of the work of Barth, Blau, and other influential figures. At stake is the question of the legitimacy of explaining exchange activity as the result of factors governing the behaviour of individuals. It is true that the researcher studies particular individuals—their strategies, actions, and the choices they make—but the ultimate focus should be on a wider sphere of activity. The reason for this is that individuals are not voluntarily involved in or relatively unrestrained by their social systems and cultural settings. It bears repeating that exchange behaviour takes place in some sort of social context through which benefits become available. In the case of politics, leaders do not make decisions in a vacuum. Leaders cannot act with impunity, especially when the material benefits of others are at stake. It follows from this that leaders and followers alike must adjust their own interest in some fashion to the interests of others, because our own interests are frequently modified to a large degree, or changed outright, by the interest of more powerful people.

In this context, because some interests are apt to hold sway over others, we can conclude that not all interests contribute equally to the emergence of social, political, and economic arrangements. As far as individual decision-making and small-group processes are concerned, the relationship between these processes and the wider social systems in which exchange takes place should be given greater attention in anthropology. The decisions made by ORG leaders, for example, cannot adequately be explained without a corresponding analysis of the wider system involving native/government interaction over economic development issues. In all, small-group activity is influenced, or even governed, by the wider system of affairs even to the extent that these wider systems will play a role in determining the content of small-group interaction and the conditions under which it exists.

(3) *Exchange behaviour has an historical dimension.* The broad historical factors which influence the structure of exchange relations are an important consideration. Since there is a tendency in anthropology to examine the decisions of individuals in isolation from the wider processes which impinge upon them, there is a corresponding tendency to neglect the ongoing historical factors which give rise to such phenomenon. In fact, it is Barth's tendency in *Models of Social Organization* to regard exchange behaviour as a logically closed system, and his inattention to wider historical processes could lead to the same errors of analysis as functionalist studies, of which Barth is quite critical.

As it stands, anthropologists need to know about the historical process by which exchange relations are transformed over time. In the Collins case, this task has been facilitated by a concern with changes which have marked Indian/European relations in the area of economic exchange, and by a focus on historical processes leading to the economic incorporation of native life into a wider system of dependency relations. The preceeding analysis, for example, discusses three different phases of exchange relationships that have characterized native/white interaction over the last three centuries. In the first phase trading took place in the context of reciprocal gift-giving ceremonies. This initial period is one of "ceremonial exchange" in which Europeans are heavily dependent upon the goods and services of the local native population. The second phase was characterized by a more direct exchange of furs for trade goods, by "trading chiefs" at first, then on an individual trapper basis. This second period involves a more direct commercial or commodity exchange, partly because traders are better able to provide for their own provisions, thus lessening their dependency on the native people of the area. By the twentieth century there was a more complete transformation to what has been termed "non-reciprocal exchange," where Europeans assume an ascendancy position in native/white relations. Such an analysis allows for a perspective on Collins political and economic activity as a developing reality, and not as an isolated set of events located at a point in linear time. Such an analysis also helps to reveal the mechanisms for the progressive concentration of power by Eurocanadians in northern areas, and offers some insights into the mode of interaction and exchange between the two groups in the future. In sum, exchange is best thought of in terms of a systems approach or an evolutionary sequence of change and not as a set of discrete, discontinuous, or isolated events.

(4) *Exchange behaviour has a cultural context.* Lest it be forgotten, it is important to acknowledge the intellectual debt that anthropology

owes its founding fathers. This is particularly true for Marcel Mauss whose book, *Essai sur le don* (The Gift), deserves to be more widely recognized for its contribution to the shape of anthropology today. Mauss's theme, that social relations are strengthened by repetitive interaction based on the exchange of goods, services, and other benefits, has provided a foundation for the later work of Lévi-Strauss, Barth, and Blau, among other influential thinkers. It is to Mauss that we owe the idea that the maintenance of society greatly depends on the reciprocal interaction of its members, such that "Food, women, children, possessions, charms, land, labour, services, religious offices, rank—everything is stuff to be given away and repaid" (Mauss 1954: 11). All in all, it was Mauss's research that provided the necessary basis for widespread comparisons of exchange behaviour.

Mauss's contribution, however, could have been greater had there not been a flaw in the way he thought about social life. This flaw, stemming from Durkheim and shared to some degree by Lévi-Strauss, mistakenly seeks the underlying patterns of social life in vaguely defined psychological tendencies. Whereas Lévi-Strauss attempts to understand the basic forms of exchange by a search for "certain fundamental structures of the human mind" (1949: 108), Mauss finds social behaviour understandable in terms of "collective representations." As far as Mauss is concerned, "All these institutions [of exchange] reveal the same kind of social and psychological pattern" (1954: 11).

We must acknowledge, of course, that in Mauss's day he did not have the benefit of the numerous, wide-ranging ethnographic studies now available to researchers. If he had, Mauss might have had less reason for seeing in exchange behaviour the same kind of pattern from society to society. From today's perspective the anthropologist, on the basis of extensive ethnographic comparisons such as that produced by Sahlins (1965), now sees a fairly close association between a society's economic and food-producing systems and the predominant form of exchange behaviour practised by its members. Thus, a range of different exchange behaviours can be perceived—from the "generalized reciprocity" of hunting-gathering bands to the commercial, monetarized exchange of industrial societies.

The point of this discussion is that cultural and socio-economic context makes a difference to the type of exchange behaviour that is found in a society. This point is also crucial to our understanding of the Collins case. Collins people retain a close proximity to their traditional hunting-society roots. In such societies leadership is based on experience and demonstrated generosity. The people who have things, such as food or tools, are expected to share them with less fortunate members of the community.

Leadership in Collins, and the ways in which benefits are distributed by the Ogoki River Guides organization, are an extension of this hunting group pattern. Collins leaders succeeded, in part, because they had the necessary rewards to distribute to followers. But more importantly, they succeeded because they were able to distribute the economic benefits over a fairly wide range of the population. Such a tactic not only served to satisfy the traditional/cultural norm of generosity; it also served to obviate divisive tendencies in Collins and to promote a more cohesive effort in the pursuit of community goals.

Maturity, generosity, and organizational skills are characteristics congruent with traditional leadership concepts among the Ojibwa and, from ORG's position, validate its authority in local affairs. In many native communities today leadership tends to be weakly developed because the chief is no longer the principal distributor of goods to his people, but in Collins its leaders have managed to maintain a key role in the local distribution of goods and services. Such a locally-controlled distribution network lends credibility to village leaders, and provides the organizational basis through which their authority can be extended and consolidated. In fact Dunning has noted, in his study of the Pekangekum village, that in Ojibwa society there is an extremely limited set of mechanisms for integration of the community as a whole. It is for this reason that he argues that special attention should be given to the role of exchange and gift giving "as the only institutional means for integrating and maintaining relationships outside the sibling group and the range of patrilateral kinsmen" (Dunning 1959a: 156). It is because of the need to study the cultural context of exchange that I have suggested that the Ogoki River Guides organization resembles an elaborate gift-giving machine, inspired along traditional ideals and sentiments, but geared to contemporary economic realities.

In summary, the discussion thus far has been an attempt to explain the role that exchange theory has played in my research at Collins. It has tried to show some of the ways that my observations and conclusions reflect the theoretical research on the topic of exchange behaviour. The summary of previous research on this topic in anthropology has shown an emphasis on the individualistic, actor-oriented approach to exchange behaviour (Barth, Blau), or on the psychological properties that underly patterns of exchange (Lévi-Strauss, Benedict, Mauss). It has been argued that while a focus on the individual performer can yield insights into exchange behaviour, this approach must be complemented in various ways with other more important considerations—the social, cultural, and historical factors that are responsible for choices that individuals make. It is for this reason that a change in direction is called for in the anthropological study of exchange. A new approach is suggested, one in which exchange behaviour is regarded as a multi-faceted phenomenon. Exchange behaviour is really only understandable as an aspect of social behaviour, having an historical sequence through time, and taking place in an identifiable cultural context.

Leadership and Community Development

The factors which help to account for Collins's economic growth fall into two general categories. One of these is the leadership the community has enjoyed over the years. The McTavish brothers in particular are bold, dynamic characters whose leadership styles facilitate successful negotiations. In turn, the development of ORG was made possible mainly by their father's material and social capital. It's hard to imagine ORG coming to exist if there had been no store in Collins. In this case some of these able persons would probably have found success in the outside world. Their ability to operate in the outside political and economic world, in contrast to the average Collins resident, has made the McTavish brothers a virtually indispensable factor in the community's development. The second general category includes the various material and social resources that the McTavish group were able to utilize in order to promote ORG activities and to provide rewards to their followers. These two areas then—leadership and available resources—define the parameters of Collins's development. From the point of view of the mid- to late-1970s, it was premature to call the Collins venture "an economic success." The lodge at Whitewater Lake was not expected to be in full operation until the mid-1980s, and a faltering economy in the rest of North America would have an adverse effect on attempts to attract tourists to northern Ontario. Collins people also have numerous plans for improving their community—roads, new houses, hydro hookups, indoor plumbing—and it will be years before one can assess the impact that these new projects, if they occur at all, will have on the population. Nevertheless, we are still left with the burden of explaining why the Collins community has made significant gains, even of a preliminary nature, while other similar settlements in the region have made no plans for the future, are still dependent on welfare, and have chronic unemployment problems. In all, surrounding communities resemble Collins as it existed in the late 1950s. Collins has changed, the others have not—the question is why?

The answer involves the interplay of a number of factors which can be divided into two main groups. In the first group are the *primary* factors which contribute directly to the success or failure of projects; these are the crucial driving forces behind the achievement of development goals. In Collins the factors most responsible for successful goal achievement are a centralized decision-making body, an overall development strategy with concrete priorities, and an effective system for the distribution of economic benefits at the local level. The second group comprises the *secondary* factors which involve the conditions or environmental situations favourable to the attainment of development goals, but are not determining factors in their own right. The ongoing process of social change, and a new access to outside resources, are the main "conditioning elements" which promoted Collins's goals.

Internal Social Processes.   When the trapping economy of northern Canada went into decline in the 1950s two processes occurred almost simultaneously—a sharp rise in both unemployment and transfer payments. But unemployment, despite its negative connotations for development, meant that a large labour force existed for projects aimed at minimizing costs by avoiding expensive labour-saving technology. As a general rule this suggests that in situations of high unemployment, operations aiming at the maximum use of local inputs have the greatest chances of success. However, it also suggests that a converse situation may occur—a labour shortage if the project succeeds, which would then require upgrading technology in order to become competitive outside the region. The Collins project did experience labour shortages in the construction phase, but this was not a long-term problem because workers could be hired from outside the community. When peak labour requirements were over, outside people were layed off first, thus maintaining relatively high employment levels for the Collins work force.

The second process was an unprecedented increase in outside subsidy during the 1950s in the form of relief, pensions, and allowances of various sorts. An increase in transfer payments, and a new accent on individual earning and purchasing, were responsible for the emergence of the nuclear family as the basic unit of social organization and for a decrease in the range and functions of the traditional kinship network. The isolation of the elementary family from extended kinship ties was also a pivotal factor in leaders' attempts to reorganize the Collins population—from horizontal links uniting various kin groups, to the development of vertical links between leaders and followers. In addition, this reorganization was facilitated by the fact that White Sand and Nipigon House people opted to establish affinal alliances with members of the more dominant Fort Hope group. This process allowed for a wide basis of "peripheral" political support, and an increased gravitation of households around local leaders.

Available Resources.   Despite Collins's isolated, relatively impoverished situation, the community did have access to three important resources which facilitated its development efforts—an attractive and rich physical environment, people with expert knowledge on how to best use this environment, and an external government willing to provide financial backing. The Whitewater Lake area was well chosen as the site for a tourist lodge. It is uninhabited for at least fifty miles in all directions, has large stands of virgin timber, and the waters contain a wide variety of fish in large numbers. The Collins people know how to travel and subsist in this boreal environment, and their skills are marketable. As such both ecological and human factors combine to form the basis for an effective tourist-oriented strategy. The third resource beneficial to Collins development was external funding and technical expertise. Such aid consisted mainly of grants and loans from various government agencies for projects within the village and at the Whitewater lodge site. For the first half of the 1970s outside financial aid amounted to about $700,000. On a per capita basis this works out to nearly $100 per person per month, or about one half as much as one could expect from unemployment insurance benefits. Put another way, 40 households receiving $325 a month in welfare would cost the government more than it dispersed through grants for Collins projects.

The problem that this sitution presents is that there is a common understanding among people from developed countries that large inputs of cash are the best remedy for underdevelopment. Given this perception we are compelled to consider the importance of outside capital in the pursuit of Collins's socio-economic goals. As a starter it would be useful to ascertain the possibility of Collins people building a tourist industry on their own, albeit on a less grand scale than eventually materialized. Their main problem would probably be a shortage of working capital, but this would be overcome using existing assets. The store complex, and additional property in a neighbouring town, could be mortgaged. If a site close to the rail line were chosen people could use their own boats and snowmachines, and thereby cut transportation costs. Construction materials available locally (logs, sand, rock) would not involve a major expense. There were enough unemployed people in the community to comprise a sufficient work force. They would have to be convinced to donate their labour, but other communities have carried out successful development projects on this basis (Barrett 1977, Knight 1978, Salisbury 1970). Collins people are not lacking in the skills to construct and manage tourist facilities in the bush. When all things are considered it is not unreasonable to conclude that Collins people were certainly capable of building a tourist industry using their own resources, and that external aid contributed to the achievement of their goals but was not a determining factor. But whether the Collins people would have actually struck out on their own without this aid remains a separate matter. Given the dynamic leadership in the community, I think they would have given it a try.

Centralized Local Powers.   In order to understand more fully the importance of political leadership in the Collins community an historical perspective has been adopted in this study. From such a perspective it becomes clear that the Collins leadership has evolved through three rather discrete stages. In the trapping period leadership was highly fragmented. Each trapping group was largely an autonomous unit, and even within these groups individual trappers took pride in making their own decisions about where to go, what to do, and how to do it. With everyone in the bush for most of the year the fur trader was not able to exert much influence, but with a change to more permanent settlement near his post, the trader's role in community affairs would become much more important.

The second stage begins with the attempts of the Collins fur trader to centralize power and authority in the village. Among his many activities, the trader dispensed jobs and services, controlled the flow of goods in and out of the settlement, and became an effective intermediary with the outside world. The main drawback was that the trader's leadership was essentially an exercise in personal influence, and there are limits to what one person can achieve alone. The emergence of ORG in the 1970s signalled the beginning of the third stage, one where community leadership consisted of a centralized administrative structure with specialized leadership roles: an organizer to plan the economy and structure the labour force, a promoter to cultivate outside interest, and a business manager to direct the cash flow and maintain accounts. It was largely because of this trend towards increased differentiation of political authority and economic power that ORG became an effective tool in the pursuit of community development goals.

Coordinated Development Strategy.   While the emergence of a centralized decision-making body greatly facilitates development efforts, such a body is no more than an elaborate tool—much depends on how the tool is used and the ends to which it is directed. What makes the Collins case different from other communities in the area is a comprehensive strategy for development, and a strong administrative body to implement it. In fact, ORG was created in direct response to the community's need for an overall structure capable of implementing the tourist lodge strategy, and thereby furthering the people's wider development goals. And when the federal government announced its Local Initiatives Program in the early 1970s Collins had a well-developed infrastructure for effectively exploiting these new resources. It took some time for the people in other neighbouring settlements to see the advantage of such an infrastructure, but by the time they started to organize, if at all, the grant program had been largely disbanded. Because of their foresight Collins people prospered, while their neighbours floundered in indecision.

Wide Distribution of Economic Benefits. When Collins people were able to integrate a number of small projects towards the achievement of a central goal, such as when a recreation grant to clear snowmobile trails was used to construct a winter cargo road to Whitewater Lake, they were able to minimize wasted efforts and funds. Ironically, they were able to achieve what the government program could not— use LIP and OFY funds to establish projects of long-term significance. In addition, this comprehensive approach helped to consolidate support for ORG on the homefront, inasmuch as workers felt a sense of continuity from project to project, and therefore from pay cheque to pay cheque.

Since most workers in the community were employed on various ORG projects at one time or another, the ingroup/outgroup syndrome, where various factions fight for exclusive control of new benefits, did not emerge in Collins. Given the limited resources available from the outside world, Collins leaders chose to disburse the benefits in a parsimonious manner, by hiring as many workers as they could while the funds lasted. If they would have used the funding to only hire a few people on a full-time basis, an ensuing struggle for local control would likely have resulted, which would have seriously threatened the community's long-term development goals. By contrast, a wide distribution of economic rewards obviated divisive tendencies in Collins and promoted a more unified effort in the pursuit of community objectives.

Development by Government Financing

While ORG owes part of its success to the strengthening of leader/follower solidarity at the local level, the cultivation of relationships outside the community have been equally important. External financing, I concluded earlier, facilitated the development efforts of Collins people, although it was not a sole determining factor in success. In all, outside funding tended to propel the village in a direction that already had been partially dictated by pre-existing priorities and organizational efforts.

Rather than overstress the contribution of external financing to community development, a more accurate approach might stress the symbiotic relationship that exists between northern Ojibwa, who have the knowledge and labour power to operate tourist facilities but lack adequate financing, and government planners who can supply cash but not the expertise. In this sense the plans of each party are essential to the plans of the other, although this mutual contingency aspect of outside-financed development is not often recognized, especially in government circles. The government or aid-giver, acting on the assumption that its own agency provides the funds which make local development possible, is apt to assert more control over community projects than the situation actually warrants. On the other hand, the aid-recipients are likely to feel a distant sense of involvement in such projects, especially when they are denied rights to the ownership of equipment, buildings, and other property accumulated with the help of outside money. The idea that both outside agents and local people are equal partners in development is largely negated by an imbalance in the power that one group is able to exert over the other.

In Collins, and in the North generally, very little property is actually owned and controlled by the native people themselves. They do not have title to the buildings and equipment at Whitewater Lake, and the provincial government has not indicated when, if ever, such property might be turned over to Collins people. A similar situation also exists in reserve communities where the Minister of Indian Affairs has the ultimate right to decide on the disposal of a band's assets. Since Collins and most other non-reserve communities are situated on crown lands, the government also exercises considerable authority over these people as well. Besides the government, the only other major property owner in the northern Ontario area is the Canadian National Railway which was given thousands of acres in right-of-ways almost immediately after the signing of Treaty 9. The fact that railway surveyors had already chosen the land most favourable for their needs before the treaty was signed (Collins 1906), probably means that both the government and the railway expected little resistance on the part of the native inhabitants. Indian people who are ridiculed for "squatting" near the railway or on crown land are acutely aware of the irony of this situation. There is no question about which party received the better deal, or for that matter about why the land transaction turned out the way it did. If the historical analysis presented earlier in this study is any indication, Eurocanadians over the past few centuries have consistently sought control over native peoples' behaviour, especially when there was an opportunity for material gain (see Stymeist 1975: 81-87). It is not surprising then that native people should lay part of the blame for their problems on an inadequate access to marketable resources and mortgageable property, and should become politically active around these issues.

In many northern areas this political activity takes on a rather distinctive form—outside agents and local people struggling back and forth for the right to make the final decisions. Continued intransigence on the part of outside administrators over this devolution-of-control issue strengthens the native resolve for increased autonomy in local affairs. Because of this political environment, "development" for native people has an added dimension. It has now come to mean more than a higher standard of living; development has become a means by which to achieve the wider native goal of self-determination. But it is debatable whether or not this is a realistic expectation because, if native people reach the conclusion that externally financed development has the net result of increasing their dependence on the outside world, then they have a right to ask if "development" has actually taken place. Certainly when a government agency reserves ownership rights in the instruments and products of development projects it is reserving much more. By retaining ownership rights the aid-giving agency also reserves the right to decide how local resources shall be utilized, and this right is a source of power over people who depend on them for their livelihood.

Collins as a Competent Community

Collins is an example of a community presented with opportunities for development which its members have effectively used to promote local interests. The skills and capabilities of community members have been used to marshal both internal and external resources, to define goals, and to organize its members in the pursuit of community objectives. The importance of community competence, or the capability for collective action and constructive response, has been recognized by various authors. Warren, for example, discusses "the capability of local people to confront their problems effectively through some type of concerted action" (1977: 538). Drawing on a wide range of community studies, Bowles indicates that in order "to actively influence or control events the community as a collective must have or develop the internal competence to manage local resources and bargain with external organizations" (1981: 57). As such, community competence involves an ability on the part of its members to define, defend, and develop the interests and aspirations of the local population. Competence, therefore, depends on a capability to identify the problems and needs of the community, to establish goals and priorities, and to develop the means and expertise to implement objectives.

The Collins case illustrates how leadership in a northern native community can effectively control and direct development projects so as to maximize local benefits, or what Bowles (1981: 57-62) refers to as

the "political efficacy of a community." A community with high political efficacy is able to act in an effective manner in dealing with internal
problems or external centres of power; one with low political efficacy is
least able to control outside pressure. Collins leaders have always
maintained that the leadership structure that has been developed in
their community is the one best suited to meet local needs and objectives, but this has caused conflicts with outside authorities. The problem is that Collins leadership, which is mainly focused around ORG, is
not structured along the representative democratic links characteristic
of the larger Eurocanadian society. This has been a source of conflict
because government officials do not view ORG as a legitimate form of
local government and have exerted pressure on Collins leaders to
adopt a more "democratic" format. This was the case when ARDA
officials initially refused to fund the ORG tourist lodge project because
they said that ORG was not a "public" body, that is, that ORG was not
a legal municipal political structure with elected representatives. The
reaction of ORG leaders was that ARDA officials were simply attempting to disqualify Collins' tourist lodge project on technicalities, and
that ulterior motives were involved. But ORG would not give up
without a fight, and so its leaders took their story to a reporter for the
Globe and Mail in Toronto. Shortly thereafter an article on Collins
appeared outlining the government's refusal to help northern Ontario's "dying Indian communities." ARDA was obviously embarrassed by the story, and a short time after, a joint DREE-ARDA press
release announced that ORG would be given a grant to begin construction of its tourist lodge at Whitewater Lake. The Federal Minister in
charge of DREE explained that the "DREE-ARDA grant had been made
possible by a new, broadened interpretation of the DREE-ARDA
agreement. This new interpretation allowed, for the first time in Ontario, a non-profit corporation to represent a rural population of Native
extraction where no municipal structure exists to take advantage of the
DREE-ARDA Agreement."

Within a year, Collins leaders were again feeling the effects of
external pressure to change ORG's role in community leadership. In
1975 the Ontario Government tabled the Northern Communities Act
(Bill 102) in an attempt to incorporate what it referred to as "unorganized communities" into the present structure of municipal government. The government's position was that some form of legally
recognized municipal organization was necessary for the provision of
basic social and physical services. In what might be termed "government by dangling," Ontario promised increased local services (power,
water, sewage disposal) for those communities willing to adopt the
idea of elected community councils. Collins leaders worried that exter-

nal manipulation would increase if they approved the idea. Essentially they suspected that the government really only wanted to increase administrative control in those areas of the province where its influence is least felt, and that government officials were attempting to create bureaucratic links through elected councils which they would ultimately control through provincial statute.

Actually there is a larger issue at stake in the Collins/provincial government conflict: Which groups, local or outside, should have the right to decide on appropriate forms of community representation? The emphasis in the Eurocanadian political process tends to be along lines that produce conflict. The structure of elections and formal votes automatically casts some people in the role of winners and others in the role of losers. One result is that the non-native political process tends to promote division rather than unity. The consequences for northern native society of adopting an adversarial political format, as Dacks summarizes, is that "Where a degree of unity can be achieved among northerners, political colonialism may well continue to fade. However, where consensus cannot be reached, pressing social and economic problems are likely to persist; conflict is likely to intensify" (1981: 88).

Similar concerns over the effects of conflict politics on Indian communities have also been expressed in a recent nation-wide study of native leaders' attitudes towards political status (Boldt 1981). As one leader phrased it, "The Canadian democratic system is totally alien to native people. The old way was true democracy . . . traditional ways had better results than modern democracy." In a similar vein another leader commented, "No, it's [Canadian democracy] alien to Indians. It divides the Indians into factions. I have seen it happen on Reserves" (Boldt 1981: 548-49). For Ojibwa Indians, the "traditional way" was to accord authority to individuals with the most experience and expertise. Leadership was based upon skill as a hunter and trapper, on maturity, wisdom, and guidance (Rogers 1965: 267-75; Smith 1973: 13-21). In other words, leadership had to be validated above all by performance. As Bailey explains: "It is a matter of creating confidence. The transactional leader works to create a kind of legitimacy for himself: to make other people expect that he will do what he says he will do. In other words [the group of followers] . . . is pervaded by faith: that the leader can deliver the goods. This faith is reinforced when the leader does in fact deliver" (1969: 76).

In fact this is precisely the point made by the leaders of ORG in countering the government's attempt to promote the idea of elected councils. The view in Collins is that ORG has earned the right to represent the community by delivering jobs and other benefits. Experience and proven organizational abilities validate ORG's authority in Collins's local affairs; abilities which are also congruent with traditional leadership concepts. A primary concern of the ORG executive is that regular elections will allow access to local positions of power by individuals who lack appropriate skills. The result could be the pervasive factionalism characteristic of many elected band councils on Indian reserves, an undermining of ORG development priorities, and possible dispersal of community members. Of course these are hypothetical consequences, since Collins has never had an elected community council, but many people in Collins presently feel that the stakes are too high, and possible benefits too low, to embark on such a venture.

In sum, the people of Collins would probably agree with Dacks's statement that Indians "see the breakdown of northern native society as far from natural and inevitable, but rather as the result of governmental manipulation" (1981: 96). Essentially they see the fate of their people as determined by federal and provincial policies that have taken their land away from them and imposed alien cultural norms on them (see Friedl 1950). The present system of elective leadership in Canadian Indian bands represents an institution that was alien to the pre-contact political practices in the Indian communities. Rather, an elected chief and council is the result of government edict, as specified in the Indian Act, and is a principle that has been in force only since the various treaties were signed with the Indian bands. Government representatives often wonder why elected band leaders have so little influence in the internal affairs of their communities since, after all, it is his band members who have voted him into that role. Part of the answer is that outside authorities "have taken over the role of leader, or attempted to do so, inhibiting the development of local Indian leadership. In addition, many of the duties of the former leaders have been stripped away ... thereby weakening their position" (Rogers 1965: 280).

The Collins community is not under the direct control of any governmental agency, as is the case with DIAND's authority over Indian reserves. The actions of ARDA officials, and those trying to legislate the "unorganized communities act," have made Collins people suspicious that their present autonomy in local affairs will also be "stripped away" by governmental edict. External manipulation, they feel, will undermine their capability for collective action and constructive response, as has already happened on many Indian reserves, and therefore will ultimately lead to the demise of their community. In Collins, ORG has forged a legitimacy for itself by providing benefits for the local population. The leaders of ORG have developed an ability to make decisions, to formulate goals, and to articulate plans for coping with future challenges; all of this is thought to be acceptable and valid by the people of Collins. Thus, ORG has come to be seen as a valuable and necessary local institution upon which ride the hopes for survival of the Collins community in the modern world.

ORG: A Model for Native Community Development?

Lest the preceding discussion give the impression that the corporate model of ORG is transferable in a general sense to all native communities, it is important to reflect on the various conditions under which such a transference would be appropriate and useful. In the first place it is worth indicating that Collins's corporate approach has had a certain measure of success because the community itself has certain characteristics which favour this approach over others. We would expect then, that the ORG model for development would be more applicable to a native community that shares more, rather than less, of Collins's main features.

The first point has to do with the characteristics of Collins leaders themselves. The McTavish brothers are largely motivated by community objectives, rather than by personal economic gain. They tend to view the Collins community as somewhat of an extension of their own family, thereby promoting an egalitarian, sharing ethic in the distribution of jobs and other benefits. Finally, the brothers' success was greatly facilitated by their ability to operate efficiently in the outside world as well as in the local community. It is these sorts of leadership characteristics which lend themselves to a political system where authority is accorded to individuals with experience and expertise. These characteristics also tend to obviate demands for formal elections and votes by dissenters who may feel disadvantaged by the existing system.

The leadership structure of ORG is, moreover, a workable format because Collins is a community only partly out of the bush, and therefore in a sense it is but half way into the modern world. It is a community which retains a close proximity to its traditional roots. Its members still follow a socio-political system where leadership must be validated by performance, where leaders rise and fall according to their ability in providing rewards for followers. In such a system leaders are not voted out of office. Dissenters can simply withdraw their support by packing up and leaving for the camp or settlement of a more suitable candidate. In communities like Collins where lots are not owned and where houses are not bought or sold but simply abandoned when no longer needed, there is a much greater ebb and flow to local populations than in areas where substantial material investment can keep people tied to particular locations.

This brings us to another important consideration regarding the size and homogeneity of the Collins population. Previously in this study certain socio-political divisions of the population were discussed, such as band membership, religious affiliation, and treaty status. The conclusion was that these divisions have not been especially important in the political arena because they have not provided the basis for the formation of special interest groups or factions capable of competing with the current leadership organization. In fact, since Collins is a non-reserve native community, it does not make much difference if one has status as an "Indian" or not, since such status does not form the basis for a differential distribution of benefits at the community level. By the same token, band membership has only a symbolic importance since Collins people do not normally participate in the social, political, and economic affairs of the "bands" to which they nominally belong.

This does not mean that Collins people lack a common identity. The younger generation has nicknamed their village "Hollywood," perhaps because they see it as a sort of "soap opera place" where a lot of social activity takes place. They also regard themselves for the most part as *Anishenabek*, as Indian- (Ojibwa) speaking people, distinct from Eurocanadians to the south and Cree to the north. They are also on the whole more than a little proud of the community effort it is taking to construct the wilderness lodge which attracts such important visitors as the premier of the province. People are working and have pay cheques to spend. This is all in contrast to the neighbouring community of Armstrong, population about 300, which saw half of its population leave when the radar base closed. This has contributed to a feeling of ascendency among Collins people when Armstrong residents must come to them for work. All of these factors have drawn the Collins people closer together than is typical of other nearby places. Collins is sufficiently structurally integrated and culturally homogeneous that the multiplicity of interests and points of view that characterize large and more urbanized southern native communities are not present, or at least not to the same degree.

The implication, then, is that the large southern reserves would probably function better with the elected council system, because after two centuries or more of contact with non-natives the council system is no longer "alien" in such communities. But in the small, more isolated native communities that are spread throughout northern Ontario, Quebec, and other regions of the boreal forest belt, there is not the same lack of proximity to a traditional political form that among southern natives was probably already forgotten by their grandparents. As such the corporate model, exemplified by Collins' ORG, is probably more adaptable to the small northern community than the large southern one.

Collins's corporate approach to development should therefore be given consideration as an alternative form of community representation. It could also be given the encouragement to develop by government agencies in northern areas where the people would like to try a different system for achieving community objectives. Of course there are certain things that are not transferable, because these must come from within, such as the local initiative and will of a people to persevere in the face of adversity.

Collins Ten Years After

When I left Collins at the end of my original field trip in 1975 I wondered what the future would hold for this place of small log cabins and large aspirations. Would the people of Collins abandon their life in the bush, or would they continue their struggle into an uncertain future? What would become of the Ogoki River Guides venture—would it dwindle into disinterest, or would its members take up the challenge of new goals and opportunities? When thinking about Collins's long term prospects I also had to keep in mind how fragile a community of only one hundred and fifty people can be, and kept wondering if ORG would collapse under the weight of its own momentum.

Now, in the mid-1980s, we have the benefit of a decade of hindsight. During this time I have maintained my interest in Collins and have made frequent return trips ranging in duration from a few days to a couple of weeks, usually during the summer months but also once or twice in the winter. There have been exciting times, such as when a terrifying forest fire burned its way to within a few miles of Collins. The women and children were evacuated by train to Sioux Lookout, and for the next two-and-a-half weeks I joined the men in a nervous vigil. I'll never forget the strange ghost-town-like atmosphere of the place, or the bizarre red and orange glow to everything—trees, water, even people—as the sunlight pressed through the layer of smoke and ash hanging overhead. There have also been sad times, such as the passing of many of Collins's elderly residents who were among the most truly generous people that a person could hope to know. Or the time that I struck up a conversation with a young woman while waiting beside the tracks for an early morning train. She pointed up to an abandoned house on a hill overlooking the rail line and explained that she had spent the last few nights staying there and now had to leave because she was hungry. I then realized that she was one of the half-dozen or so children that used to live in the house during my first period of fieldwork. Her parents had both died, she explained, and her younger brothers and sisters were placed in foster homes. She had come home for a last, albeit lonely, visit.

I am also sorry to relate that Collins's oldest building, the store and trading post, burned to the ground one January night after a newly installed oil furnace sprung a leak. Luckily there were only two occupants of the building at the time, John and Tom McTavish, both of whom survived the ordeal. With his brother yelling at him to wake up, John was forced to jump from a second story window, with only his jeans on, into the snow banks below. Imagine standing barefoot in the snow, with the temperature near −20 degrees, watching everything you own go up in smoke. However, despite this tragedy the McTavish brothers in characteristic fashion were quick to rebound from adversity. John and his family moved into his brother Tom's two-bedroom cabin near the lake, a new store was set up in the old school house, and before long the family was able to carry on as usual.

One can easily talk about many other such personal events because it is events dealing directly with changes in people's lives that tend to stand out. But for the settlement as a whole, the most important changes occur in the organization and institutions of community life. Among the more important changes in this regard in the last decade are the great strides taken by Collins people in transforming the local educational system. Previously I discussed the serious problem that confronted the community when there were more students than could be accommodated in the one-room school house during a particular year. Since it was the Department of Indian Affairs that built and managed the school and hired the teachers, officials in this department decided that only children with treaty status would be allowed to attend—Métis and non-status Indians would have to find another way to receive an education. This decision was not acceptable to the majority of Collins's people, so they decided to boycott the school until such time as a solution could be found that would allow all children, status and non-status, to attend the same school. A temporary compromise was then worked out such that all children enrolled up to grade six would be allowed to attend the local school, while those in grades seven and eight would be sent out to school in Thunder Bay, some one hundred and sixty miles to the south. But it did not take long before the worst fears of the parents were realized. Within weeks many of these students had run away and hitchhiked back to Collins.

The parents of these children became increasingly upset with the manner in which this crisis was being handled from the outside. From their perspective, uncaring bureaucrats were dividing the people along status lines, and had been instrumental in ruining the school year for many of the grade seven and eight students. The parents resented having so little control over this situation, and were determined to do something about it. In a dramatic turn of events, Collins people, led by the McTavish brothers as leaders of ORG, decided that the only solution was to take matters into their own hands. Their first task was to bring about a change in the jurisdiction of the Collins school—from the Federal Department of Indian Affairs to the Ontario Ministry of Education. It was felt that the Ontario Ministry would be more responsive to Collins needs and would have no reason for dividing the people along status lines. Since Collins does not have status as an official Indian reserve, even though the majority of its residents have retained their rights as status Indians, one suspects that the Indian Affairs Department would also be pleased to rid itself of an ambiguous and troublesome situation. Given the existing dilemma, the transfer of jurisdiction went smoothly despite the initial hitch caused by the Ontario Ministry insisting that Indian Affairs bear the educational costs of status Indians in Collins. Eventually an agreement was reached, although understandably the parents were not pleased with the prospect of having the education of their children jeopardized by another Federal-Provincial dispute.

The next step in Collins's attempt at gaining more control of their affairs was the formation of a local school board. At first the Ontario Ministry refused to allow such a move, as its official argued that the population of Collins was too small to have its own board. The Ministry had decided that the Collins school would be administered by the Lakehead Board of Education in Thunder Bay. Of course this decision did not please Collins residents who insisted that the formation of a local school board was an essential step if positive changes were to be made in the Collins educational system. The parents were tired, they argued, with having unsympathetic outsiders control educational affairs in Collins on the assumption that local people were not capable of doing the job themselves. Despite the Ministry's decision Collins people went ahead and formed their own school board. They then braced themselves, expecting a long struggle over the matter.

To their surprise, instead of criticism and confrontation, members of the Bernier-Stokes School Board, as it is now called, found Ministry officials receptive to their plans. On the whole, the Ministry was pleased to find people interested in the development of local education. Buoyed by this initial success, school board members began drawing up plans for a new school building. The style and design was to be similar to the tourist lodge at Whitewater Lake, especially in the use of a horizontal log construction and an "open concept" interior. With the help of a Ministry architectural advisor, blueprints were drawn up and the new school completed by autumn 1981. In comparison to the one room tin shanty with its constantly peeling paint and frozen water pipes that served as the Collins school for twenty years, the new school is an impressive structure. Roughly circular in shape, its shiny pine logs seem almost an extension of the surrounding forest. It has well-furnished classrooms (including two computers and a TV Ontario satellite dish), and a large open play/instructional area. The school boasts two modern wood/oil furnaces, ceiling fans for effective heat distribution, thermal windows and other features suited to the northern climate.

These developments in Collins are important not only because of the pride that parents and children show in their school, but also because the Collins situation stands in contrast to other native communities in the North where such things as broken windows and on-going school vandalism are a serious problem. Parents in such places almost never visit the school and absenteeism is consistently high. One is compelled to ask why the situation should be any different in Collins.

There is no single answer to this question, but one of the main reasons is that Collins people, out of sheer frustration more than anything else, have taken the initiative in attempting to gain more control over what happens in their community. The formation of a school board in Collins was a pivotal step, since it has allowed local people the power to hire and fire their own teachers. Previously, with Indian Affairs doing the hiring, most of the teachers sent to Collins were recent graduates who needed a job for certification and who owed their allegiance to officials in some distant headquarters. Once they were certified, such teachers tended to return to their home communities in southern Ontario, resulting in a lack of continuity from year to year for the students of northern centres. For the first time, Collins people have the power to choose the teachers that they feel will make the best contribution to the development of the local school system. Teachers, too, have a different attitude when they realize that they are primarily accountable to the local population—for the first time parents and teachers have started to work together.

While this change in Collins's educational system is probably the most significant development over the last decade, it is also important to indicate that its residents have been active in other areas as well. Besides the new school, a number of other construction projects have taken place, including a new community hall, teacherage, Anglican church and rectory, all using the same pine lodge construction. As Table 18 indicates, Collins people have continued to be successful in obtaining outside funding for special projects. Such projects have been a steady employment source for Collins people, as well as providing an opportunity to experiment with different construction designs and techniques. After a shaky start, the tourist lodge at Whitewater Lake is gaining new customers each year, although at present it is still operating near the break-even point of about 40 percent capacity. Initially the leaders of ORG tried to operate the lodge themselves, but they found that they could not do this job properly and still devote attention to the various on-going projects in Collins. It is for this reason that for the last three years the lodge has been leased to individuals who operate two other lodges in the area. However, the lodge still hires Collins people as guides and maintenance workers, thus fulfilling one of the main reasons for the construction of the lodge in the first place.

TABLE 18

Collins's New Buildings: Capital Funds

	Amount ($)	Source
School (1981)	100,000	Ontario Ministry of Education
Teacherage (1983)	58,000	Ontario Ministry of Education
Community Hall (1982)	30,000	Canada Works Programme
Church and rectory (1980)	10,000	Anglican church and community members

Besides these construction projects, Collins people are preparing for the future in other ways. The village site has now been surveyed, and streets, in design at least, have been laid out. Where formerly Collins residents were squatters on Crown land, they now have their own lots and pay school taxes. But even greater changes are expected in the near future. For some time logging roads have been making their way towards Collins and one of the last large stands of timber left in Ontario. The road is now only about ten miles away, and while Collins people are not afraid of this development, you can sense a mood of nervous anticipation in their voices. With the road will come cars, more strangers, and changes that most people have scarcely dreamt about. But with the continued inspiration of leaders such as the McTavish brothers, the people are looking at this development in a positive light. They are looking at it as an opportunity—to open a sawmill, to generate profit, to provide additional jobs, and so on. With ORG still at the helm, Collins can be expected to survive the precarious transition from bush squatter to modern northern community without coming apart at the seams in the process.

References

Attwood, D. W.
1974   Patrons and Mobilizers: Political Entrepreneurs in an Agrarian State. *Journal of Anthropological Research* 30: 225-41.

Bailey, F. G.
1969   *Strategems and Spoils: A Social Anthropology of Politics.* Oxford: Basil Blackwell.

Baldwin, W. W.
1957   Social Problems of the Ojibwa Indians in the Collins Area in Northwestern Ontario. *Anthropologica* 5: 51-123

Barrett, S. R.
1977   *The Rise and Fall of an African Utopia.* Waterloo: Wilfrid Laurier University Press.

Barth, F.
1959   *Political Leadership Among the Swat Pathans.* London: Athlone Press.

1966   *Models of Social Organization.* Royal Anthropological Institute, Occasional Paper No. 23.

Benedict, R.
1959   (orig. 1934) *Patterns of Culture.* New York: Mentor Books.

Biggar, H. P.
1924   *The Voyages of Jacques Cartier.* Ottawa: Publications of the Public Archives of Canada, No. 11.

Bishop, C. A.
1974   *The Northern Ojibwa and the Fur Trade.* Toronto: Holt, Rinehart and Winston.

Black, M. B.
1969   Eliciting Folk Taxonomy in Ojibwa. In S. Tyler (ed.), *Cognitive Anthropology.* New York: Holt, Rinehart and Winston.

Blau, P. M.
1964   *Exchange and Power in Social Life.* New York: John Wiley.

Boas, F.
1897   *The Social Organization and the Secret Societies of the Kwakiutl Indians.* Washington: Report of the U.S. National Museum, 1895.

Boissevain, J.
1966   Patronage in Sicily. *Man* 1: 18-33.

Boldt, M.
1981   Enlightenment Values, Romanticism, and Attitudes Toward Political Status: A Study of Native Leaders in Canada. *Canadian Review of Sociology and Anthropology* 18 (4): 545-65.

Bowles, R. T.
1981   *Social Impact Assessment in Small Communities.* Toronto: Butterworths.

Brody, H.
1975   *The People's Land: Eskimos and Whites in the Eastern Arctic.* Harmondsworth: Penguin.

Champlain, S.
1907   *Voyages of Samuel de Champlain.* W. L. Grant (ed.), New York: Barnes and Noble.

Codere, H.
1950   *Fighting with Property.* Monographs of the American Ethnological Society, 18. New York: J. J. Augustin.

Collins, W. H.
1906   On Surveys Along the National Transcontinental Railway Location Between Lake Nipigon and Lac Seul. *Geological Survey Department of Canada*, Sessional Paper No. 26: 103-9.

Dacks, G.
1981   *A Choice of Futures: Politics in the Canadian North.* Toronto: Methuen.

Dunning, R. W.
1959a   *Social and Economic Change Among the Northern Ojibwa.* Toronto: University of Toronto Press.

1959b   Ethnic Relations and the Marginal Man in Canada. *Human Organization* 18: 117-22.

Duran, E. C. and J. A. Duran
1973   The Cape Croker Indian Reserve Furniture Factory Project. *Human Organization* 32: 231-42.

Durkheim, E.
1938   (orig. 1895) *The Rules of Sociological Method.* New York: Free Press.

Easton, D.
1972   Some Limits of Exchange Theory in Politics. *Sociological Inquiry* 42 (3-4): 129-48.

Elberg, N., R. F. Salisbury, and J. Hyman
1975   *Not By Bread Alone: The Use of Subsistence Resources Among the James Bay Cree.* Montreal: McGill Programme in the Anthropology of Development.

Ellis, C. D.
1960   A Note on Okima·hka·n. *Anthropological Linguistics* 2: 1.

Friedl, E.
1950   *An Attempt at Directed Culture Change: Leadership Among the Chippewa, 1640-1948.* Ph.D. Dissertation, New York, Columbia University.

Gearing, F. O.
1960   *Documentary History of the Fox Project*. Chicago: University of Chicago.

Godelier, M.
1971   "Salt Currency" and the Circulation of Commodities Among the Baruya of New Guinea. In G. Dalton (ed.), *Studies in Economic Anthropology*. Washington, DC: American Anthropological Association.

Hawthorn, H. B.
1966   *A Survey of the Contemporary Indians of Canada, 1*. Ottawa: Queen's Printer.

Hedican, E. J.
1982   Governmental Indian Policy, Administration, and Economic Planning in the Eastern Subarctic. *Culture* 2 (3): 25-36.

Henriksen, G.
1971   The Transactional Basis of Influence: White Men Among Naskapi Indians. In R. Paine (ed.), *Patrons and Brokers in the East Arctic*. St. John's: Memorial University of Newfoundland.

Henry, A.
1969   (orig. 1809) *Travels and Adventures in Canada and the Indian Territories Between the Years 1760 and 1776*. Edmonton: Hurtig.

Innis, H. A.
1970   *The Fur Trade in Canada*. Toronto: University of Toronto Press.

Jorgensen, J. G.
1971   Indians and the Metropolis. In J. O. Waddell and O. M. Watson (eds.), *The American Indian in Urban Society*. Boston: Little, Brown and Co.

Kapferer, B.
1976   Introduction: Transactional Models Reconsidered. In B. Kapferer (ed.), *Transaction and Meaning*. Philadelphia: ISHI.

Knight, R. K.
1978   *Indians at Work: An Informal History of Native Indian Labour in British Columbia*. Vancouver: New Star Books.

Landes, R.
1937   *Ojibwa Sociology*. New York: Columbia University Press.

Lévi-Strauss, C.
1949   *The Elementary Structures of Kinship*. Paris: Presses Universitaires de France.

Lips, J. E.
1947   Naskapi Law (Lake St. John and Lake Mistassini Bands). *Transactions of the American Philosophical Society* 37 (4): 379-492.

Lowie, R.
1920   *Primitive Society*. New York: Boni and Liveright.

Malinowski, B.
1961   (orig. 1922) *Argonauts of the Western Pacific*. New York: Dutton.

Mauss, M.
1954   (orig. 1924) *The Gift*. New York: Free Press.

Miller, W.
1955   Two Concepts of Authority. *American Anthropologist* 57: 271-89.

Morantz, T.
1982   Northern Algonquian Concepts of Status and Leadership Reviewed:
         A Case Study of the Eighteenth-Century Trading Captain System.
         Canadian Review of Sociology and Anthropology 19 (4): 482-501.

Paine, R.
1971   A Theory of Patronage and Brokerage. In R. Paine (ed.), *Patrons and
         Brokers in the East Arctic*. St. John's: Memorial University of New-
         foundland.

Ponting, J. R. and R. Gibbins
1980   *Out of Irrelevance: A Socio-Political Introduction to Indian Affairs in
         Canada*. Toronto: Butterworths.

Ray, A. J.
1974   *Indians in the Fur Trade*. Toronto: University of Toronto Press.

Rogers, E. S.
1962   *The Round Lake Ojibwa*. Toronto: Royal Ontario Museum.

1965   Leadership Among the Indians of Eastern Subarctic Canada. *An-
         thropologica* 7: 263-84.

Sagard-Théodat, G.
1936   (orig. 1865) *Le Grand Voyage du Pays des Huron*. Paris: Chez Denys
         Moreau.

Sahlins, M.
1965   On the Sociology of Primitive Exchange. In M. Banton (ed.), *The
         Relevance of Models for Social Anthropology*. London: Tavistock.

Salisbury, R. F.
1970   *Vunamami: Economic Transformation in a Traditional Society*. Berkeley:
         University of California Press.

1977   Transactional Politics: Factions and Beyond. In M. Silverman and
         R. F. Salisbury (eds.), *A House Divided? Anthropological Studies of Fac-
         tionalism*. St. John's: Memorial University of Newfoundland.

Skinner, A.
1911   Notes on the Eastern Cree and Northern Saulteaux. *Anthropological
         Papers of the American Museum of Natural History* 9: 1-177.

Smith, J. G.
1973   *Leadership Among the Southwestern Ojibwa*. Ottawa: National Museum
         of Man Publications in Ethnology, No. 7, National Museums of
         Canada.

Spindler, G. and L. Spindler
1971   *Dreamers Without Power: The Menomini Indians*. New York: Holt,
         Rinehart and Winston.

Stymeist, D. H.
1975   *Ethnics and Indians: Social Relations in a Northwestern Ontario Town.*
        Toronto: Peter Martin Associates.

Thwaites, R. G. (ed.)
1896-   *The Jesuit Relations and Allied Documents: Travels and Explorations of the*
1901   *Jesuit Missionaries in New France, 1610-1791.* Cleveland: Burrows
        Brothers.

Usher, P. J.
1976   Evaluating Country Food in the Northern Native Economy. *Arctic* 29
        (2): 105-20.

Warren, R. L.
1977   The Good Community—What Would It Be? In R. L. Warren (ed.),
        New Perspectives on the American Community. Chicago: Rand McNally.

Index